Body and Blood

Formission
Rowheath Pavilion
Heath Road
Bournville
Birmingham B30 1HH

Body and Blood

The Body of Christ in the Life of the Community

ANDREW R. HARDY
and KEITH FOSTER

CASCADE *Books* • Eugene, Oregon

BODY AND BLOOD
The Body of Christ in the Life of the Community

Copyright © 2019 Andrew Hardy and Keith Foster. All rights reserved. Except for brief quotations in critical publications or reviews, no part of this book may be reproduced in any manner without prior written permission from the publisher. Write: Permissions, Wipf and Stock Publishers, 199 W. 8th Ave., Suite 3, Eugene, OR 97401.

Cascade Books
An Imprint of Wipf and Stock Publishers
199 W. 8th Ave., Suite 3
Eugene, OR 97401

www.wipfandstock.com

PAPERBACK ISBN: 978-1-5326-5731-3
HARDCOVER ISBN: 978-1-5326-5732-0
EBOOK ISBN: 978-1-5326-5733-7

Cataloguing-in-Publication data:

Names: Hardy, Andrew R., author. | Foster, Keith, author
Title: Body and blood : the body of Christ in the life of the community / Andrew R. Hardy and Keith Foster.
Description: Eugene, OR: Cascade Books, 2019 | Includes bibliographical references.
Identifiers: ISBN 978-1-5326-5731-3 (paperback) | ISBN 978-1-5326-5732-0 (hardcover) | ISBN 978-1-5326-5733-7 (ebook)
Subjects: LCSH: Missions—Theory | Missions | Church and the world | Christianity—21st century | Christian life | Theology, practical
Classification: BV4520 H373 2019 (paperback) | BV4520 (ebook)

Manufactured in the U.S.A.   06/07/19

Scripture taken from the Holy Bible, REVISED STANDARD VERSION. Copyright © 1946, 1952, 1971 by the Division of Christian Education of the National Council of the Church of Christ in the USA. Used by permission. All rights reserved worldwide.

Scripture taken from the Holy Bible, NEW INTERNATIONAL VERSION®, NIV® Copyright © 1973, 1978, 1984, 2011 by Biblica, Inc.® Used by permission. All rights reserved worldwide.

Formission
Rowheath Pavilion
Heath Road
Bournville
Birmingham B30 1HH

We would like to dedicate this book to our families who have supported us as we have engaged in research and writing. This book is also dedicated to all of those brave missional pioneers who whilst praying "Thy kingdom come" are willing to "get in the mix" of the "local" as Christ's ambassadors.

Contents

Preface | ix
Acknowledgements | xiii

Chapter 1
Community Lifeblood—So What Is It? | 1
—Keith Foster

Chapter 2
The Missional Community Needs a Body | 8
—Andrew Hardy

Chapter 3
Entering the Conversation within
the Post-Secular City | 26
—Keith Foster

Chapter 4
Equipping Post-Secular Missionaries | 33
—Andrew Hardy

Chapter 5
So Who Are the New Marginalized? | 45
—Keith Foster

Chapter 6
Grounded Theory, Methods, and Means of Embodying Jesus
among the New Marginalized | 50
—Andrew Hardy

Chapter 7
The Importance of Place in Community | 71
—Keith Foster

Chapter 8
**Shaping New Sacred Places
in a Post-Secular Atmosphere | 77**
—Andrew Hardy

Chapter 9
**A Case in Question—Enhancing Community
and Talking Jesus | 98**
—Keith Foster

Chapter 10
How Phoenix Church Equips Urban Missionaries | 108
—Andrew Hardy

Conclusion
So What Now? A Hopeful Future | 129
—Keith Foster

Appendix
**Does the New Testament Expect All Believers
to Engage in Mission? | 133**

Bibliography | 136

Preface

The idea for this book came about in a conversation that Keith and I had together during one breakfast meeting in Coventry in 2016. Keith shared an idea for a book that would be focused on the body and lifeblood of Christ. He suggested we could write it together. It would focus on how the church needs to be brought to life in its work in the city through drawing on its social capital. This immediately resonated with me. I had long been thinking of writing a book on how the church may be viewed as a vehicle that equips believers to participate in the ongoing mission of Jesus in community-development projects in cities. In this introduction you will first hear what Keith has to say about his reasons for writing this book. I will then finish with a brief description of my own motives.

Keith's Comments

While I may not be a medical doctor, the past eighteen months or so have taught me that lifeblood (the blood that flows through our arteries and veins), is important and complex. With several elements (red cells, white cells, platelets, et al.) all performing a different function and each needing to be at a healthy level, any increase or reduction in any of these elements can cause problems. They can even be life-threatening. I learned this from being diagnosed with a form of blood cancer in the summer of 2016. Polycythemia Vera (PV) is a condition where due to a gene malfunction (the JAK2 gene to be precise) the bone marrow over-produces. Working in overdrive, too much blood is produced leading to a dangerous, potentially fatal level of platelets. So why would I introduce a book about how the local church might engage with its local community with something that may be more at home within a medical journal? Well, just as our bodies have lifeblood comprising of various elements that collectively impact the quality of the life we live, communities can also be said to possess "lifeblood." This "lifeblood" can also be measured by various things and can seriously impact the overall well-being of a community. In partnership with my friend and colleague Dr Andy Hardy, this book seeks to ask how the local church as the body of Christ might positively impact its local community lifeblood. Borne out of our collective doctoral studies, this book will bring a perspective from both church and community and will hopefully energize the reader into motivating their local church body into seeking to enhance the life of their local community.

Andy's Comments

I believe that the missional church conversation needs to pay more attention to the sacramental nature of the missional body of Christ. The Lord's Supper is one of the sacraments. The church is called the body of Christ by Paul[1] as well as the loaf (bread) of Christ.[2] It might be said that Christians are a sacramental people sent out into the world to offer the bread and wine that is the life-giving knowledge of Jesus the Savior to all who will receive him. It would also seem fitting to suggest that the Holy Spirit might be likened to the life-giving presence of Christ that flows through the very spiritual veins of every believer, as well as being at work among those who as yet do not know Christ. As a spiritual theologian, I take this very seriously. If our churches (the body) are not acting as facilitators that help us to discern God's voice (the lifeblood) calling us to participate in God's mission in broader society, then it would

---

1. 1 Cor 12.
2. 1 Cor 10:14–17.

Preface

seem that the Eucharist has not performed its primary role. This primary role is suggested by Paul to pertain to the remembrance of the Lord's death until he comes.[3] In other words, this book focuses our attention on how the missional body of Christ at its best would seem necessary to equip every believer to become participants in the divine mission as they follow the Spirit of Jesus at work ahead of and alongside them.

Defining Key Terms

It is important to define what the writers mean by lifeblood. They use it in two quite different ways in this book. Keith identifies it with social capital. His use of this term is social scientific rather than theological (see on chapter 1). I use the term blood, or lifeblood, to refer to the work of the Spirit, including the Spirit's work in the lived in and embodied expressions of social capital invested in a community, which people can draw on. It is in life that is lived that social capital is invested and drawn on. I believe that the Spirit is at work in the social and relational matrices of the world, as well as in the life of people who inhabit the social structures that organize the way we all behave (see on chapter 2). My definition of lifeblood includes Keith's concept of social capital but, whereas, he is only using sociology to define it, I use theology.

Both of us hope and pray that God blesses you as you journey with us in this book.

Andy Hardy and Keith Foster
December 2018

---

3. Luke 22:19; 1 Cor 11:26.

Acknowledgements

We would like to acknowledge the input of members of Phoenix Church into some of the research findings taken from fieldwork. We would like to also acknowledge the helpful feedback on versions for chapters from Lesley Foster, Jenny Hardy, Michelle Savage, Pam Davis and Donald Morton. Additionally the helpful editing work of Chris Mason.

Chapter 1

Community Lifeblood
—So What Is It?

KEITH FOSTER

Introduction

Home is where the heart is. This familiar saying reflects the inner longing of each of us to belong; to know what it is to be part of a place, a community that we might recognize and call home. Lesslie Newbigin, the great missionary to India and pioneer of what many call the missional conversation, defined the gathered community of God's people as the "hermeneutic of the gospel." This, according to Newbigin, is a community characterized by praise, truth, hope, community concern, mutual concern, and service.[1] Newbigin recognized that there was something special about community, particularly a community of God's people who could model what it was to follow a new master, King Jesus. The apostle Paul could acknowledge this inner desire to belong when writing to the church at Rome, to those "called to belong to Jesus Christ."[2]

1. Newbigin, *The Gospel in a Pluralist Society*, 227.
2. Rom 1:6.

Whatever our background, whatever our religious persuasion, community matters. The solution to Dorothy's dilemma in the classic film *The Wizard of Oz* was to remind herself that "there's no place like home."

Leonard Hjalmarson captures this in his book *No Home Like Place*, urging the rediscovery of the importance of place in both our theology and lived-out communities. Social scientists have for many years identified this important aspect of community wellbeing. Early pioneers such as Bourdieu, Coleman, and Putnam led the way in speaking about social capital, what we feel about our communities, that sense of community-belonging, dependency.[3] And in more recent years, Chris Baker has led the way with regards to theology entering the conversation.[4]

This book seeks to both enlighten and challenge the urban-facing church and the everyday believer. It aims to enlighten in the sense of informing and bringing up to speed with the "conversation" so far between social science and theology; but also to challenge readers to seek not only to understand but also to incarnate and enhance the "lifeblood" of our communities.

This all said, an early caution is necessary. This is not an exercise in informing a more robust social gospel. Out of an unashamed evangelical paradigm, my desire is that this book will equip the church of believers not only to understand better and enhance their local sense of community, but also unapologetically to do that while declaring the good news of the life, death, resurrection, and return of King Jesus, the only hope.

Social Capital—Measuring Our Communities

"Not everything that can be counted counts and not everything that counts can be counted." This is a saying accredited by some

---

3. E.g., Bourdieu, "The Forms of Capital"; Coleman, "Social Capital in the Creation of Human Capital"; Putman, *Bowling Alone*.

4. Chris Baker has written many books, journal articles, and papers: Baker and Skinner, *Faith in Action*; Baker and Miles-Watson, *Exploring Secular Spiritual Capital*.

to the great theoretical physicist Albert Einstein, by others to the sociologist William Bruce Cameron. Whoever said it first, this is a true saying. Many things in life are of supreme value, yet cannot be counted per se. A recent UK credit-card advertisement hinted at the same when it recognized that many things are considered to be "priceless" (showing pictures of relationships, high achievements, family reunions, etc.), yet at the same time promoting its card for the purchase of everything else. Social capital seeks to measure the "priceless," the things that cannot easily be counted, yet count all the same. The UK Office of National Statistics has sought to categorize what the varying elements of this "community lifeblood" (social capital) might be, measuring things such as personal relationships, social support networks, civic engagement, trust, and cooperative norms.

In his 1995 landmark article "Bowling Alone," US political scientist Robert Putnam made a direct and causal connection between the increasing isolation and individualism in US society and the breakdown of community, both in a visible and felt sense. People were choosing to bowl alone, watch sport alone with the fascinating subject of me, myself, and I chipping away at their community sense of us and we.[5]

Others such as Anne Power and Helen Wilmott divide this "sense of community" (social capital) into two main categories, bonding and bridging capital.[6] *Bonding* capital being our personal connections—how we connect, trust, and rely on others in our community. *Bridging* representing our organizational ties and sense of belonging—to the local play group, school, church, craft club, etc. Bonding and bridging capital each, according to Power and Wilmott, contributing to our sense of local belonging. So, if Newbigin's claims of the power and hope of the community of God's people are true, how might the church as the hermeneutic of the gospel enter the local community and enhance the lifeblood, sharing its values and qualities of hope, truth, mutual service, and such like? As Chris Baker suggests, a good place to start might be

5. The article was later expanded into a book: Putnam, *Bowling Alone*.
6. Power and Wilmott, *Social Capital within the Neighborhood*.

for the church to actually join the local conversation,[7] yet for that to happen, suspicions on both sides might need to be recognized and addressed.

Theology—Joining the Conversation

The relationship between social science and theology has been a tentative and delicate one to say the least. Indeed, theology has tended to have been viewed with suspicion within many quarters of the academic world. Those whom have bravely ventured into projects within these joint arenas can face harsh criticisms from proponents of each discipline. While the insights from social science can provide valuable and practical approaches and methodologies for the researcher, the perceived barrier for those viewing it through an evangelical biblicist lens is to be found where "often the account given about a given subject is more informed by social science than by theology."[8] Add to this the emphasis of many practical research projects on empirical research techniques and data, it can be easy to see how joint socio-scientific and theological projects within the field, known as practical theology, could be perceived to be "under the spell of social science."[9] This can then discourage community-facing churches from researching or "getting to know" their local communities. There is a school of thought within many evangelical churches that "the gospel is the gospel," with any research activities or attempts at contextualization being seen as leading to the potential "watering down" of the life-saving message of salvation and new life through Christ. The purist form of this may be the street preacher, shouting out their evangel accompanied with evangelistic handouts, giving little thought to the recipient's circumstances.

Several years ago, I was walking through my local city center when someone with such an approach thrust a tract into my

---

7. Baker, *Spiritual Capital and Progressive Localism*.
8. Cartledge, *The Use of Scripture in Practical Theology*, 280.
9. Cartledge, *The Use of Scripture in Practical Theology*, 281.

hand whilst at the same time exhorting me to turn to Jesus and "repent!" Despite my polite attempts to inform him of my passion and love for Christ, my words fell on deaf ears, he had his method and he was going to stick to it! In contrast, many years previously, in my first paid ministry role as a Community Pastor, I worked on an estate in Portsmouth where I had lived for more than twenty years. The local stories and folklore were familiar to me. Our girls had grown up in the community, attended the local playgroup and schools. For a number of years previous to this, I had also worked part-time for the local youth service, working with local teens in council-funded youth clubs. This all led to a deep and rich understanding of local culture and community, both of which would stand me in good stead as I entered local community ministry.

Opportunities for ministry were manifold; local schools, community boards, the local healthy living center, all opened their doors and welcomed me into the community "conversation." This "permission," I would like to think, had been earned over years of incarnating, being with, caring for, and sharing the ups and downs of being part of the "local" life of this community. My challenge to the local community-facing church would be to maximize their influence, incarnate as broadly and widely as the Spirit leads and permits. Many of us live in multi-cultural communities where there is a broad range of worldviews; to categorize whole communities as postmodern, secular, or other, is naïve to say the least. Many people from varying backgrounds now enrich our communities, many of whom will possess some sort of theistic (God-based) worldview.

It is vital that the evangelical church, as "the hope of the world," sees the opportunity and value of bringing theological and spiritual insight into such communities. Stephen Pattison suggests that theologians (and I would add the local church and church members as "ordinary" theologians) have a great deal to offer the secular academy (and local community), specifically with its "insider" knowledge of the increasingly diverse spiritual and religious communities that many of us find ourselves living in. As already stated, many of our communities have become diverse racial and religious mixes of varying people groups, with many possessing a theistic worldview. The secular academy needs to understand such communities and cannot ignore such large pockets and groups of theistic colonies if they too are to maximize their understanding and related interaction with people within them on a professional or social level of engagement. Theologians and the local church can be of great help as they offer insights into such faith-based communities, whether it be in the identification of beliefs, myths, metaphors, and symbols, or transformational and reflective knowledge, or even perhaps detailed theological insights into theistic worldviews and associated behaviors. Pattison states:

> The challenge for all seeking human well-being is to recognize this religious component of existence and to see how it can be integrated into an overall quest for human flourishing.[10]

A fine balance on both sides of the research community needs to be sought, one that Mark Cartledge and Stephen Pattison argue has not yet been achieved.

One theologian who has been prepared to take the risk here is Professor Chris Baker. He is leading the way with regards to asking how theology might enter the community conversation. My brief conversations and meetings with Chris have been invaluable as I seek to encourage my evangelical counterparts to join me in seeking to enhance local community lifeblood; yet doing so with a gospel intentionality. In addition to the secular academy's definitions of bonding and bridging capital, spoken of by the likes of Power and Wilmott, Baker has defined his own categories of community well-being (social capital) out of the theological academy, speaking of spiritual (the church's motivation to action, or the "why") and religious (the form such community input takes, or the "what") capital.[11] Together, according to Baker, spiritual and religious capital provide the motivation and outlet aimed at enhancing the lifeblood of our communities. Adding to these, Baker

---

10. Pattison, *The Challenge of Practical Theology*, 202.
11. Baker, *Spiritual Capital and Progressive Localism*.

speaks of the importance of identifying those equivalent, yet not necessarily faith-based, motivations found within our local communities. This secular spiritual capital, according to Baker, can be found in many people within our communities who equally seek the well-being of their local "place." Such a meeting of faith-based (spiritual capital) and non-faith-based (secular spiritual capital) peoples can lead to what Baker further defines as a progressive localism, as people come together with a common goal for the common good.

While Baker's emphasis is around seeking "better communities," this book unashamedly seeks to motivate Christ's followers from within the evangelical tradition to enter the community conversation, with the joint aim of enhancing local community life yet doing so with a gospel intentionality that is loyal to the four evangelical values identified by David Bebbington.[12] This means an approach that not only seeks to communicate the good news of Jesus in active projects (activism), but one that sees the message of the cross as central to all it does (crucicentric). It also sees the Bible informing its approach and strategies (biblicist) with a desire to see local lives transformed for Christ and his kingdom (conversionist). While "better communities" is an honorable goal, Tim Chester's caution is an important one, warning that better communities without gospel declaration and motivation can simply become "signposts pointing nowhere."[13]

---

12. Bebbington, *Evangelicalism in Modern Britain*.
13. Chester, *Good News to the Poor*, 65.

Chapter 2

The Missional Community Needs a Body

Andrew Hardy

Introduction

In the last chapter, Keith introduced us to some common themes that will need to be explored and fleshed out in this book. He finished by implying the need for the contemporary church to engage in more than the social gospel. He argued for the need to engage in an evangelical missiology that is shaped by gospel intentionality. If it does not then it is in real danger of losing the primary focus of the gospel of Christ. Having said this, we will need to carefully consider what we mean by gospel intentionality. The four themes of evangelical practical theological and historical identity were mentioned in the last chapter, as well as how these need to remain an important theological narrative to help frame and inform the missiological integrity of the evangelical tradition. In this chapter, I will discuss how the spiritual capital of evangelical mission would seem to require that faith communities of this tradition equip every person to have a consciousness of themselves as participants in the mission of God. This has often not been the case in the evangelical sector.

God Creates a People with an Identity

I listened to Jane and Peter tell the story of how they had been inspired by the example of the founding leader of their church to plant a missional community in their house. This leader had begun their church ten years earlier. They were now seeking to do the same thing in their home and neighborhood. What had impressed them was his deep love for Jesus and his commitment to help others in his neighborhood by forming friendships with them (i.e., drawing on gospel intentionality and local social capital of which this leader had earned a part). This couple had accepted Christ about five years earlier because of his work with them. Now they were doing the same kind of things he had modelled to them. He had spoken often about his conviction that he was doing what Jesus had done with his first disciples. Their story had been informed by their leader's journey in missional ministry, as well as by his narrative theology grounded in Jesus' life and ministry. These influences had helped them to develop a consciousness of themselves as followers of the Christ, who they believed to be still at work in the world.

We all have stories that we use to define who we are. These stories act a bit like scripts we use to inform us of who we are in the context of our life-experiences. This is true of the stories that we have constructed in our minds that help us to discern where we come from, why we are here, what the meaning of life might be, and what we think our destinies and futures might hold for us. Many Christians also have a big overarching story that they locate themselves within, in which they learn that they were created by a God who has a purpose for their lives. This purpose was thwarted because of humanity's choice to break their covenant relationship with God. The majority of theologians call this "the fall." It is believed by many evangelicals that this led to the presence of evil entering into this world, providing numerous competing counter-narratives aimed at the subterfuge of the gospel of the kingdom metanarrative.

Through Jesus Christ's life, death, resurrection, and return to God, the Triune God[1] may be said to have made it possible for humans to be reconciled to God. This requires Jesus to be genuinely accepted as Lord. Yet it requires much more than the initial choice to accept Christ. Scripture calls us to follow him for the rest of our lives. One of the goals of the mission of God includes the final eschatological reign of God to be established. Missiologists like Lesslie Newbigin suggest that we are actually participants through the Spirit of Christ in this cosmic mission.[2] This implies that each of us need to subject ourselves to engage in a lifelong faithful relationship with God.

So it might be suggested that the people of God need to frame and inform their identities in the light of the bigger missional story found in the Bible. Christians most often learn how to follow Jesus in the context of Christian communities (churches). Paul called such communities "the body of Christ" (1 Cor 12). How might our Christian communities equip believers to intentionally participate with the Spirit of Jesus in what he is inviting them to do alongside him? The body of Christ might be said to have been enlivened by the lifeblood of the Spirit of Jesus. It might be claimed to provide each believer with an interior experience of Christ's presence.[3] By becoming sensitive to the inner promptings of the Spirit, each of us might learn to more empathetically identify the work of the Spirit in others, who are also on a journey seeking to find Christ. It might be said that Christian communities can be a means of extending the hospitality and generosity of God to others. The most practical way to become part of a community is to seek to meaningfully interact with our neighbors. It will also encourage us to be active community participants who contribute to the social capital of a community. We need to earn our place in it.

---

1. Father, Son, and Holy Spirit.
2. Newbigin, *The Open Secret*, 54.
3. 2 Cor 4:1–6.

For example, we might do this by hosting social gatherings in our homes, sharing food and offering support to those who are open to explore the Christian faith with us. This kind of thing is an important gesture of our presence and availability to others who share life in our communities. Another way of putting this is to suggest that our lives need to represent a welcoming picture of God's family to those we share life alongside.[4] Our homes may become exhibitions of God's love, generosity, and hospitality. Part of this involves introducing people to the living resurrected Jesus so that they too can become members of God's family.

The resurrected Christ's presence will be in an authentic Christian household. My use of the metaphors of the body of Christ and the lifeblood of the Spirit are what gave me inspiration to write my contributions in this book. Paul comments in 1 Corinthians 12 that Jesus is the head of the body and that each believer is a member of it. Each one of them has gifts given by the Spirit (the Spirit is the lifeblood of the body). The goal is for the body of Christ to grow and mature as its participants grow in their willingness to be vulnerable with God and each other.

A missional community needs by definition to be a place that welcomes mess, openness, and empathy aimed at allowing each of its members to be authentic and honest with God and each other. Spiritual maturity might be likened to a creative and messy art studio. If we apply this metaphor to a missional community, it could be thought of as the place where participants imaginatively share life together with the Spirit inspiring the painting of a new landscape for the lives of those who are part of it. As new people become part of God's family. The body of Christ grows and extends its influence into broader civil society. It has a kind of spiritual and social capital all of its own, which like money in a bank account can be drawn on in order to invest in those who as yet do not know Christ. These people may metaphorically be claimed to need to be able to draw on the life-giving Spirit's energizing generosity and hospitality in the context of their communities. This requires missional communities to have deep capacities that tolerate mess

---

4. Hardy, *Pictures of God*.

and allow people to participate with others in his body as the Spirit of God dwells among them.

In order to understand who Jesus Christ is and what he has done for each person, each of us need to understand the bigger story of his mission and what that means for each of us. At the most fundamental level, each believer, or not-yet-Christian, has a story of how they first met Jesus, or are on a journey of discovery to find him. These are the kinds of stories we need to share with each other. We might say it requires this kind of empathetic and messy community where people can bring real-life challenges, sharing them to then be energized to face these challenges and overcome them. This requires believers to share their stories without seeking to veneer them with a false Christianized glow, as this does not represent the actual real hardships and challenges they have faced in real-life situations. It will be these kinds of authentic, shared, life narratives that will help others to find the kind of encouragement to seek help from the God of generosity. So who are we, according to this kind of deeper revelatory story of how God is at work in our more grounded messy lives? How might we identify ourselves in the light of the big Christian story? How might our identities be framed and informed by the story of Jesus as he keeps on journeying alongside us? One important observation at this stage is that communities that welcome mess also call on each participant in them to be vulnerable in what they share of their real-life struggles.

Redefining Who We Are

Let me share a little of my story to begin this exploratory journey. I believe it has something in it that might be meaningful to at least some readers. I was brought up by good parents, but they were not Christians and they did not provide, as such, a Christian upbringing for my brother or I. In my later teens my mother became a Christian. Unknown to me, she was praying for my brother and I. At the age of fifteen, I had a vividly realistic dream one night in which I found myself in a beautiful garden. I felt like I did not belong there. I felt impure and unworthy. I had never really had an experience like this in my normal everyday life, so it had a big impact on me in the year that followed it. It happened on March thirteenth 1978.

As I looked around the garden I turned and saw an old man. I perceived that he was deeply insightful and wise. I sensed it more than anything else. He had deep penetrating eyes that seemed to pierce into the depths of my being. He asked me a question, "Andrew how long do you want to live?" As he asked this question he gave a knowing smile and nodded his head. At the same moment I felt myself being torn away from this place. I cried out over my shoulder, "wait a minute, give me a year. No sorry, give me forty years." I found myself rushing through the clouds at great speed, the wind whooshing past my body. I saw the earth below hastening up towards me, and suddenly, like a bolt of lightning, I landed on the pavement at the bottom of my best friend's road. We had fallen out with each other at the time, much to my consternation.

This dream troubled me every day for the next year. On March 13th of the following year (1979), I wondered, "Has he given me another year?" I am still here and that happened thirty-six years ago. I breathed a sigh of relief. Another year went past and my former friend one day turned up on the doorstep of my house. He asked to speak to me. I was pleased to see him. He invited me to go on a walking holiday with a group of his new friends. I decided to go. During that holiday he shared his newly found Christian faith with me. This was the same friend whose road I had landed near in my dream. A couple of months went by and Christ revealed himself to me in a remarkable way.

I was walking in the woods. It was a bright sunny day. There was a gentle breeze in the air. I invited God to reveal himself to me. I felt strongly that he wanted my permission to do this. I had questions, and the one of first importance to me was whether there was a God. I felt a presence come into me, as tangibly as if a source of immense power had hit me like electricity, lighting a bulb. One moment I did not sense this presence and the next I did. I realized that this was not something I could conjure up for myself. It was real. I found it convincing and knew at that moment God was real.

I accepted Jesus as my Lord and began to intentionally seek to find out more about him. At the moment I was filled with this presence, I also felt impelled to follow Jesus for the rest of my life. I also felt convicted to serve in some form of Christian ministry. I did not know that it was called "ministry" at that time, but sensed that I was being sent to represent Christ to others.

What is still amazing about this story to me is that God had revealed two years earlier that my friend would be instrumental in my conversion. Interestingly, his house was only about 200 yards up the road from the church in which I was to be baptized. In fact, it was in the woods that surrounded this church that I was filled with God's presence. I remember, soon after my conversion, that my mother became very ill and almost died. I spent weeks praying for her. One night after walking back from the hospital, I went into the parkland near the woods where I had experienced the presence of God. A picture appeared in my mind's eye of Jesus dying for me on the cross. He spoke to me from the cross, "Andrew you know how much your mother suffered for you as a child, I suffered for her and for you so much more." As this vision disappeared, someone in the woods started to sing a praise song. He may have also seen something, I don't know. His praise song seemed more than a coincidence.

I walked the several hundred yards from this parkland area to where I had landed in my earlier dream of the garden. I looked up into the starry night sky, I said, "Lord Jesus, I don't want to live for one year, or forty years, but forever with you." I now understood what God had really been asking me in that dream. I have gone on, since then, to be a district minister for twelve churches, including two church plants and the planting of two missional youth communities. I presently work with a missional ministry training college.

I have come to realize that *all* of the people of God have been called to follow Jesus and to become missionaries in their everyday life contexts. What Keith and I write in this book, we hope, might help readers to be equipped to participate in what God has called them to undertake. My identity is bound up in my love for the

Lord Jesus Christ. I want to follow him faithfully giving my life as an instrument of faithful service to him. It is important that each of us learn how to follow the living Lord Jesus as we are influenced by his Spirit to engage on a lifelong journey. I believe the Spirit continues to be sent by the Father to define who each of us are and what our parts might be in participation with the ongoing mission of Jesus. In other words, the story of Jesus defines our identities. His life might be thought of as a representative model of what human life is to be at its best. Christ is still at work calling us to participate with him in transforming the world.

The Missional People of God

Paul Stevens' landmark biblical study of what he considers to be the true identity of the people of God is important to any consideration of our participation in the mission of God. In his book *The Abolition of the Laity*, he argues that the New Testament does not make distinctions between ordained clergy and laity. He points out that the Greek word *laos* simply means "people."[5] In its New Testament context, it refers to the community of believers as the "people of God,"[6] whether or not they are church leaders. Thus, *all* Christ's followers should be understood as the laity, and the term "laity" needs "abolishing" as a nomenclature to describe "ordinary" (as distinct from ordained) Christian believers.[7] Fundamental to his argument is that those who are ordained to professional ministry have often disempowered the "laity," because of a professionalization of the idea of Christian service, making it particularly the property of the properly trained and educated minister.[8] He suggests that *every* person in the Christian community needs their identities redefining as "the people of God,"[9] whom God has sent

---

5. Stevens, *The Abolition of the Laity*, 56.
6. Stevens, *The Abolition of the Laity*, 54–57.
7. Stevens, *The Abolition of the Laity*, 3–23.
8. Stevens, *The Abolition of the Laity*, 24–49.
9. Ibid., 24–49.

to exercise their gifts as works of service (ministry).[10] He interestingly defines the *laos* of God as those who take their identity from the Trinity:

> A fully Trinitarian approach is needed since the identity and ministry of the *laos* is shaped by the God whose people we are. God has called out "a *laos* for himself" (Acts 15:14) or as the KJV puts it, "a people for his name." The identity of the *laos* comes from the Trinity—a people in communion with God—and the vocation of the *laos* comes from communion with God. In this way both the being and the doing, both the identity and the vocation of the *laos* will be considered.[11]

The identity of the people of God arises from the recognition that they belong to the Trinity's family. God is their Father, Jesus is their Lord and elder brother, and the Holy Spirit is the means by which Jesus continues his ministry in the world. It is the task of his people to seek to discern and participate in it in their everyday life-contexts.[12] They are a sent people, who take their identity from being equipped by the Spirit of Jesus[13] to participate in the *missio Dei* (a Latin phrase meaning "mission of God").[14] This leads Stevens to comment:

> The ministry of the *laos* is not generated exclusively by the people, whether from duty or gratitude. All ministry is God's ministry and God continues his own ministry through his people. This ministry begins not when we "join the church" to help God do his work but when we join God (Jn. 1:12) and have "fellowship with the Father and with his Son" (1 Jn. 1:3). Laos ministry is participation in the "in-going" ministry of God (relationally among God the Father, Son and Holy Spirit), and

10. Eph 4:10–12.
11. Stevens, *The Abolition of the Laity*, 56.
12. Hardy, *Pictures of God*, 73–79.
13. Acts 16:6–10.
14. For a discussion of the evolution of this Latin phrase see: Tennent, *Invitation to World Missions*, 487–89; Flett, *The Witness of God*, 123; Bosch, *Transforming Mission*, 390.

simultaneously participation in the "out-going" (sending) ministry of God. On this latter point Jesus prayed in the high priestly prayer, "as you sent me into the world, I have sent them into the world" (Jn. 17:18). On the first (the in-going) God is "lover, the beloved and the love itself," as Jürgen Moltmann puts it, reflecting on a phrase from Augustine. On the second, God is sender, sent and the sending.[15]

It is the whole people of God who are sent to be followers of Christ, shaped to be like him, and guided to participate in his mission to make authentic followers of others. In this sense, we argue that *every* believer is to be thought of as a missional minister sent by the Triune God of mission to follow Jesus. He guides us to participate in his work of discipleship, among other things, with those who as yet do not know him. Our identity as the missional people of God is that we have been sent to participate in the ongoing mission of Jesus.[16] We have been called, not so much to ask Jesus to be with us each day but rather we are called to ask him to show us how to walk in his footsteps, so that we might do what he wants us to do each day.[17]

Following Jesus means we must walk as he walked. Paul termed this keeping in step with the Spirit.[18] It requires that we receive the ability through the Holy Spirit to discern what he is calling to us to participate in doing alongside him.[19] This requires a radical reorientation of much popular Christian teaching. Among other matters, popular teaching seems to often pander to meeting the consumer needs of worshippers who require good preaching and lively worship songs as the product they pay to receive in church. There is a real danger that consumerism has made the church a provider of spiritual goods and services. The service paid

15. Stevens, *The Abolition of the Laity*, 56, 57.
16. Hardy, *Pictures of God*, 73–97.
17. Hardy, *Pictures of God*, 73–97.
18. Gal 5:16.
19. Acts 16:6–10 provides an excellent example of how the Spirit guided Paul's missionary team.

for in offerings is the care of the professional Christian minister. This seems to lead to a kind of falsified Christian consumer gospel, provided as services on a Sunday morning, rather than a missional discipleship gospel where we are all sent to serve each other and the world as Christ's representatives.

A radical reorientation is needed. The people of God need to be equipped by missional churches to be able to effectively use their gifts to participate in what God is doing in the world. The New Testament posits a picture of the people of God as sent to serve God seven days a week. This is so that we might join with the Spirit in extending the reign of God into people's life experiences. God is sovereign. He is already Lord of the whole earth.[20] It may be said that Christ calls each of us to radically re-orientate our lives to behave as Jesus behaved. He placed extraordinary value on the self-giving love of Father God. This love seemed to motivate his mission.[21]

One way we might conceive of this kind of radical gift-love is to think of the book of Acts. We observe in Acts accounts of how the early church expected to continue seeing Jesus at work in the world around them.[22] Might we not expect the same kinds of ongoing revelation of the mission and work of Jesus in our contemporary situation?

Christ equipped his early followers to make disciples of others as a participation in his own ongoing mission.[23] Each of us may come to think of ourselves as already part of God's kingdom of grace and thus called to do likewise.[24] The key questions we might need to ask ourselves are, Who is Lord of my life? How do my priorities reflect the reign of God in my life? Am I a follower of the Lord Jesus? Am I participating in his ongoing mission? We could add to this, Is your church equipping you to be a missionary with this kind of identity? As Stevens has suggested, each one of the

20. Phil 2:9.
21. John 5:19, 20.
22. Acts 13:1–3; 16:6–10, etc.
23. Matt 28:16–20.
24. Fee, *Paul, the Spirit and the People of God*.

people of God are called and sent by the Father to participate in the ongoing ministry and mission of Jesus. "Our lives are not our own," Paul declared, "You have been bought with a price, therefore serve God in your mortal bodies."[25]

If our local churches are really mission-equipping agencies, then our identities as participants in God's in-breaking kingdom will need to redefine how we see ourselves as participants in Jesus' ongoing mission. Paul used the metaphor of the human body for the Corinthian believers to illustrate how every organ is to function in contributing to the life of the whole body.[26] It is to be a unified body, guided by the Spirit of Christ. It is the risen Lord who will continue to unite each part to serve God and others.[27]

This image of the church as the body of Christ is not of a stationary statue-like figure but rather of a living, mobile organism.[28] The body of Christ is *mobile*. It is a missional body, sent by the Spirit of Christ to participate in making disciples of others. The body of Christ is mobilized by the Spirit to model to those we interact with what it looks like when Christ is part of our lives. In the first chapter, Keith informed us that the body of Christ may be termed the hermeneutic of the gospel.[29] Each person as a member of it is to be like an Auto-Theo-Biography (ATB). This ATB might

25. 1 Cor 6:20 NIV.
26. 1 Cor 12.
27. 1 Cor 12:1–11.
28. Paul's metaphor of the body is akin to that of the ancient Greco-Roman idea of the civil body of people who made up their society. It is not the same of course, but the imagery of the body politic arises in that context. The body of Christ is the new society of God's people that has a position with the ascended Christ, placing each believer spiritually in the heavens with Christ (Eph 2:6). This new society lives in between times, between the present heavens and the new heavens and earth. This new society (body) is therefore to serve an ambassadorial function (2 Cor 5:16–21). The body of Christ is mobile within present societal structures but no longer belongs to them, but has citizenship in the new kingdom society. The body of Christ is therefore an outpost and foretaste of the kingdom of God mobilized as the hands and feet of Jesus' missional body in this present fallen world, according to Newbigin, *Lesslie Newbigin Missionary Theologian*, 184, 214, 231.
29. Newbigin, *The Gospel in a Pluralist Society*, chapter 18.

be thought of as the story of each of our lives understood in terms of God's work in and through us.[30] Pete Ward uses the concept of ATB to represent how Scripture helps us to develop our Christian identities with reference to the Christian story brought together by the ongoing work of the Spirit to inspire it.[31] Paul described the lifestyles of those who had Christ in them to be like a sweet fragrance that others could smell and appreciate.[32] It is alluring and compelling to those whose spiritual senses are livened and inspired by God's Spirit.

The Mobile Missional Body

This mobile missional body of Christ may be said to embody a personal and corporate identity for the people of God. It may come to realization when each of us come to see ourselves as united with the one controlling head (Jesus Christ is the head of the body).[33]

The lifeblood of the body of Christ is the Spirit.[34] The Spirit, as the flowing lifeblood of Jesus might be said to empower people to participate in the life-giving sacrifice and new resurrection life of Jesus.[35] Resurrection life might be considered to be symbolic of the real presence of Christ.[36] In other words, as parts of the body of Christ, we are filled with the Spirit of Jesus, which is founded on the giving of his life for the world.[37] We are a sacramental body, in the sense that we represent the sacred presence of the living Jesus to those with whom we engage in mission. He is with us to the end of the age.[38] We are the body and the Spirit is the lifeblood. We

---

30. Ward, *Participation and Mediation,* 4, 18.
31. Ward, *Participation and Mediation,* 4, 18.
32. 2 Cor 2:15–17.
33. Col 1:18.
34. 1 Cor 11:23–26.
35. Rom 6:1–8.
36. Sheldrake, *Spaces for the Sacred,* 79, 81, 82–83, 86, 89, 169–70.
37. Robinson, *The Biblical Doctrine of the Church,* 55–122.
38. Matt 28:20.

are called to serve the Eucharist to the people of the world as the metaphorical hands and feet of Jesus.

In what ways does your local church equip people to identify their specific gifts so that they might exercise them whenever they sense the call of the Spirit to work alongside Jesus?

The Sacramental Body of Christ

This is what I term a new kind of sacramental missiology for the missional people of God. It is part of my theological starting point that every member might be considered an active agent of Christ. Each of us may be guided by the Spirit of Jesus as he continues his mission to bring the whole world under the reign of God.[39] We are already a part of his kingdom.[40] It might be argued that the missional body of Christ needs to reframe its identity and purpose to become an equipping agent for the followers of Christ to become this kind of sacramental missional body.

Ancient Israel as a Metaphor of the Missional Church Community and Its Life

It is interesting to note that in the book of Numbers the people of Israel were called the "community" or "congregation."[41] It is interesting to also note that when the Hebrew Scriptures were translated into Greek in the second century BC, the Hebrew word used to refer to Israel as the "community," or "congregation" of God,[42] was translated as the Greek word *ekklesia*.[43] The Greek word *ekklesia*, assembly, is used in the New Testament, especially by Paul, to refer to the church.[44] Church for Paul was understood as a community

---

39. Wright, *The Mission of God's People*.
40. John 5:24; 10:27–30.
41. Num 1:16.
42. Pickle, *The Word Church in the Old Testament*.
43. Pickle, *The Word Church in the Old Testament*.
44. Gal 1:1–3.

of believers, both Jew and gentile, joined in their identity by their faith and allegiance to the Lord Jesus.[45]

In other words, the idea of the church for Paul was framed and informed by the concept that believing gentiles and Jews alike were part of the renewed Israel, making them all part of the same kingdom of God.[46] The church is a kind of embassy representing Christ to the world. This faith-community was made up of a people (*laos*) who were all part of Israel's renewed "community" or "congregation."

This newly defined Christian people sought to participate with the Spirit of Jesus in proclaiming the good news (i.e. gospel) of the in-breaking reign of God to the peoples who lived in Roman society. To be part of the kingdom of God meant to be subject and obedient to Christ as his servants.[47] Christ as Lord was to be served.[48]

The people of God were to have the same attitude and frame of mind that Christ had.[49] He came to model what serving God the Father looked like.[50] Paul called the Philippian Christians to model their lives on Christ's example and to take on that same attitude of mind for themselves. Christ, he said, emptied himself of all claims to be God and rather became a servant to do the Father's bidding.[51]

The concept of the church as a community that already belongs to the kingdom of God[52] is fundamental to a sacramental theology of mission. The community of believers is to be the hermeneutic of the gospel of the in-breaking reign of the Triune God.[53] When faith-seeking people join with Christians in their homes, as they work alongside them in their work places, or meet

---

45. Col 1:1, 2.
46. Wright, *Paul: Fresh Perspectives*.
47. Matt 6:10.
48. Acts 2:21.
49. Phil 2:5.
50. John 14:8.
51. Phil 2:1–9.
52. As we await its final and full arrival when Jesus returns.
53. Newbigin, *The Gospel in a Pluralist Society*, chapter 18.

them in the gym, etc., there might be a sense of the good news of God's presence experienced through interaction with them. This might be called missional spiritual capital. Each of us need to be like living storybooks that others can refer to and learn about the Lord. In other words, the *laos* of God need to become living letters easily read by all people.[54]

Becoming Part of the Body of Christ

We would suggest that people will become part of the body of Christ when they meet Christ in the lived-out stories of his missional people. This requires each of us to intentionally live out our lives among them. Becoming part of the body may start with people coming to feel that they belong in missional communities that incarnate Christ among them in their neighborhoods. It could be a coffee shop, a pub, or a foodbank.

In other words, a sacramental incarnation of the mobile missional body of Christ needs to be embodied in places where people want to meet—often termed by scholars to be *third places*, or so-called *neutral spaces*. Third places will not necessarily be mobile, unless they are soup kitchens for the homeless run out of a van. Mobile mission can include the mobilization of the people of God to journey with their faith stories to live them out with people in third places that don't move, like a coffee shop.

One of the students who completed a BA degree in mission with my college now works in a coffee shop for the homeless which has become a kind of church for about two hundred of them. People like this will need to belong for quite a long time before they might start to believe, or behave in new ways as potential followers of Christ. Places like missional coffee shops may choose to invest in the communities they incarnate among, as a kind of missional venture capital, as well as a kind of provision of bridging capital. What I mean by "missional venture capital" is that, like in anything that has substance and worth in it, there is a kind of benefit that

---

54. 2 Cor 2:2–3.

can be drawn on. It is like drawing on our savings to capitalize and sustain our lives. Missional venture capital is invested with the power of the Christian story lived out rather than preached to people in third places.

It may also be claimed to be invested with the supernatural presence of the Spirit of Jesus, who is the source of all life and power.[55] Hence missional venture capital is fundamental to the bridging capital of missional ventures. People interested in Christ will hopefully be naturally drawn to the real presence of Jesus that will be at work in the friendships they forge with believers. People might start to feel like they belong in places invested with missional venture capital. They could be said to draw on the deposit of that capital invested by the people of Christ in them in the intentional friendships they have with them in third places.

Following the Head of the Body

I am making the case for a fresh way for the people of God to come to see themselves as the mobile missional body of Jesus, called to incarnate the story of the good news of the in-breaking reign of God in secular third places. In order to do this, we need a fresh kind of Spirit-given sensitivity that will need to be addressed in a later chapter. We might need to learn how to discern the work of the Spirit ahead of the church in the ordinary rounds of everyday life. This means we need to learn to follow the head—Christ—as he leads us by his Spirit.

There are many notable examples we could refer to from the Bible of how the God of mission helps his people to do this. It is worth mentioning Acts 16:6–10 at this point. In this passage, we are told by Luke how Paul was guided by the Spirit of Jesus to take the gospel to Macedonia. The story is rich in terms of the account of how the Spirit of Jesus guided Paul and his team to take the message to Europe. The reader may want to consider this passage. Perhaps ask yourself in what ways you have been guided in your life to go to where the Spirit has guided you. What does the Spirit's

---

55. For example see on John 1:4.

voice sound like? In what ways has God led you? Perhaps ask other Christian friends the same questions. It may prove beneficial to ask God to help you to learn to hear the Spirit's voice more fully in order to go on this missional journey into third places.

In order for us to follow the head of the mobile missional body of Christ, it will need to be based on a revelation of what God calls each of us to participate in doing. May God bless all of us with revelations of how he wants us to put our trust in the head of the body, so that we might faithfully serve him as his missional hands, feet, and face of compassion. Each of us may consider ourselves to have been sent to serve life-giving bread and wine to the world around us. This is indeed a fresh way to express what might be termed a new missional sacramental theology.

A proper context for exercising this kind of practice may well find one important sphere in which to undertake its labors. We might term this "the post-secular city" as our societies may well be undergoing transformation toward what might be termed post-secular.

Chapter 3

Entering the Conversation within the Post-Secular City

KEITH FOSTER

Introduction

There is and has been a great deal of talk about modernism, post-modernism, secularism, post-Christian, and even now what some are referring to as post-secularism.[1] Many people will have slipped through each of these "invisible" stages of social and theological category without feeling a thing—fish rarely think about the water they are swimming in. It could be tempting to leave the categorization of community attitudes to church and faith to the theologians and social scientists, yet it is critical for all of us engaged in mission to understand our local culture and community and to grasp how the gospel relates to that culture, how our attitudes to culture impact our approach to communicating the good news. Not knowing the stories and folklore of the people we are trying to reach for Christ can create issues. Paul and Barnabas found this out when trying to reach the people of

1. Chris Baker, Justin Beaumont, et al.

Lystra.[2] Misunderstandings and miscommunication can impact our impact. This tension between church and world, gospel and culture, has been heightened by the increasing secular / spiritual divide over the centuries.

James Thwaites in his challenging book *The Church Beyond the Congregation* suggests that the, "overriding issue within the western church is that is has been severely influenced by its Platonic, Greek inheritance which separated the sacred church from the secular world."[3] Thwaites' point is that since the transition from a faith influenced by and built upon a Hebraic platform (where God in everyday life, work, and world was the norm) to one increasingly influenced from a Greek platform (that clearly distinguished between the spiritual and the secular) in the church's attempt to define and distinguish itself as a people set apart, the church has become increasingly disconnected from society in general. With both secular society and church "pushing" each other away over the centuries, the gap has understandably widened, thus the need for a re-negotiation of the relationship. Whereas the church within a theistic society was central to the functioning and decision-making of government and community, in what some are now declaring to be a post-Christian society in the Western world, this space and place of influence has been lost. This raises some important questions for the church in the West, questions about attitudes to culture, contextual questions of gospel communication, of being a people "in the world but not of it."[4] As an evangelical Christian, I would say these are questions that the evangelical church needs to wrestle with if it is to once more impact community at every level.[5]

---

2. Acts 14:8–20. The people of Lystra had local folklore that told the story of the gods Zeus and Hermes coming to visit them. The people had not recognized them and the resulting judgment took the form of a catastrophic flood. Paul and Barnabas, having performed miracles, were assumed by the people of Lystra to be Zeus and Hermes, and thus the people started to worship them, not wanting to repeat the mistakes of their ancestors.

3. Thwaites, *The Church Beyond the Congregation,* 36.

4. John 17:14.

5. As a starter for the new enquirer, I would recommend Lesslie Newbigin's *The Gospel in a Pluralist Society*, additionally Tim Chester's *Everyday Church*.

While it would be wonderful for whole movements of evangelicals to "land on the same page" with their answers to such questions, ultimately, it may well be that each church has to carry out its own investigations and local negotiations. Either way, this is a pressing issue, no more so than in what some are referring to as the post-secular city, a window of opportunity for the church to re-enter the local community conversation.

What Is the Post-Secular City?

Chris Baker has identified a significant development in the openness of communities for faith dialogue, defining this as a progressive localism, whereupon churches and faith-based organizations are no longer considered to be restricted to their own private discussions and projects but actually have a valuable contribution to make.[6] The common community meeting ground (according to Baker) is the identification of common language and/or ethical goals, defined by what he terms secular spiritual capital or:

> . . . the set of individual and corporate/community values and actions produced by the dynamic interaction between spiritual and social capital within secular fields of activity.[7]

This broadens the community conversation out. It is no longer about the church filling the gap of governmental welfare provision, but about a common provision of place and developmental sense of community that identifies and celebrates the individual contribution and the synergy this creates for the common good. This includes all community stakeholders, both secular and faith-based, giving rise to what Justin Beaumont and Chris Baker refer to as the post-secular city.[8] The post-secular city would seem to present an ideal opportunity for the urban-facing churches to participate and even direct a new all-embracing community initiative

---

6. Baker, *Spiritual Capital and Progressive Localism*.
7. Baker and Miles-Watson, *Exploring Secular Spiritual Capital*, 7.
8. Beaumont and Baker, *Postsecular Cities*.

beyond a needs or welfare-based provision. By way of definition, Beaumont and Baker define the post-secular city as:

> A public space which continues to be shaped by ongoing dynamics of secularization and secularism . . . but that also has to negotiate and make space for the re-emergence of public expressions of religion and spirituality.[9]

This new "mood" and openness to faith-based organizations creates a fresh opportunity for urban-facing churches to take the initiative with the creation of meaningful place. Places that allow the development of both bonding and bridging capital whilst also developing more meaningful and deeper discussion (progressive localism) beyond felt and local community needs.

Elaine Graham and Stephen Lowe in their book *What Makes a Good City?* affirm the church's central role since, "Christianity has been an urban religion since its very beginnings."[10] This said, it seems that the shared community conversation between secular and faith-based organizations is still largely driven out of a welfare agenda. Beaumont and Baker acknowledge that:

> The neoliberal turn and the stripping down of the welfare state have returned us to a condition where public charity once again is called upon and charitable welfare has always been a calling of faith-based organizations.[11]

When the welfare state struggles, the church becomes popular again. This perception of the supportive role of the church is good and proper and provides great collaborative opportunity for urban community churches; but if this stereotypes the church into what Cloke suggests as some sort of neoliberal welfare provider that simply "occupies the vacuum of welfare space left behind by retreating central and local government activity"[12] then it is no wonder that churches might live up to this and seek to operate solely within

---

9. Beaumont and Baker, *Postsecular Cities,* 32.
10. Graham and Lowe, *What Makes a Good City?* 1.
11. Beaumont and Baker (eds.), *Postsecular Cities,* xiii.
12. Cloke, Beaumont, and Williams, *Working Faith,* 8.

this needy sector of their local community. Baker infers the need for the broadening impact of faith-based communities as, "an all-embracing source of energy, not only for the devout but for society in general as well."[13]

The Church beyond Welfare Provision

Churches from a whole array of denominations have sought to find a "way in" to their local communities. Motivations to do so range from the desire to reflect "God's love in action" to a broken world, through to an overt evangelistic and unashamed intentionality of gospel declaration. A significant number of such efforts are often based around and in response to the perceived or even substantially researched measured needs of the community. With the quantitative assistance of community-assessment tools and data produced by such as The United States Census Bureau[14] and the UK's Office of National Statistics (ONS),[15] the measured needs of a community can be known and utilized as a basis for subsequent program-based community initiatives without a single local conversation needing to take place. Couple this together with an emotional appeal, such as the New Testament book of James, which points out the futility of words of blessing without action,[16] then it can be all too tempting for churches to "swing into action," seeing themselves as agents of kingdom blessing addressing a needs-based agenda. Where the need is within a church program, that's where the focus of the people and finance can often be—the squeaky wheel often gets the oil.

This has led to many new community-focused ministry roles appearing alongside more traditional ones within church periodical vacancy sections as churches seek to employ someone to "lead the charge" into the needy local community. Many such

13. Beaumont and Baker, *Postsecular Cities*, 5.
14. https://www.census.gov/.
15. The ONS produce regular census statistics on a broad number of measures—including deprivation: https://www.ons.gov.uk/search?q=deprivation.
16. Jas 2:14–17.

roles can be billed as some sort of "community vigilante," hired to "get into the mix" of a church's local tough estate. Such estates or communities are often portrayed as "hard" or "marginal" places.[17]

Yet what about the (perceived) unmarginalized? How might the church seek to create places for conversation that are designed to reach and engage with those outside of the measured gaze of such as the ONS? A 1985 report by the Church of England called *Faith in the City* was written to challenge the Church to, "become local, outward looking and participative."[18] With a focus on deprivation and inequality, the report acted as a catalyst for many to spring into action, to be agents of deprived urban reverse. To support the programmed initiatives, the Church Urban Fund was duly set up, "as a practical response to unmet need."[19] The need had been identified, the Church of England had been challenged, the funds were made available, thus the great project could begin. Yet for many, "the report was felt . . . to be profoundly deficient (in) the area of theology."[20] Gaps and questions arose with regards to faith connections with the city. Plenty was being done and planned to the city but how were faith dialogue and connections with the city being encouraged? Once the people had been "fed and watered" what was the vision "beyond freedom from poverty?"[21] Theology would be a project for another day, the urgent call for now was to get on with the task in hand, to bring relief to the urban poor and deprived.

Feeding into this was the total emphasis on measures of deprivation; the unemployed, the less well educated, the measured marginalized. After all, a quick sweep of the Scriptures would tell us that even Jesus considered it "hard" for the rich to enter the

17. Two such folk are Mez McConnell and Paul Cloke. Mez McConnell is an FIEC/Acts 29 church planter who, amongst many things, oversees the 20Schemes project aimed at planting gospel churches in needy areas. Paul Cloke has written extensively on ministry to the marginalized—just two examples of where needy = urban deprived.

18. Sedgwick, *God in the City*, 16.

19. https://www.cuf.org.uk/about-us.

20. Sedgwick, *God in the City*, 16.

21. Sedgwick, *God in the City*, 17.

kingdom of heaven.[22] A kingdom eschatology of equality and release of the oppressed was needed to counter the relentless capitalist eschatology[23] of the urban rich.

More recently, Mike Pears helpfully identified the complexity of this urban paradox, rich and poor side by side,[24] acknowledging how difficult it is to see "the close proximity of the *greedy and the needy*," with such urban places being no more than "landscapes of power."[25] For Pears, the term "marginalization" embraces both "geographical and social exclusion,"[26] one's geography and "score" on the scale of deprivation qualify you as marginalized. So, the question must be asked again, what about the (perceived) unmarginalized? Those living in the nice apartments opposite the council tower block? While many may not possess "felt" or obvious material needs, they still have needs. Following Jesus' statement about the rich and the kingdom of God, Luke immediately goes on to write about the salvation of a rich tax collector.[27] Might this challenge the many churches with a focus on the deprived to seek to reach the same? If 15 percent of a community are unemployed, what about the majority who are not? There is a danger that those outside of the ONS measured deprivation statistics can be excluded from the church's gaze too. With regards to the kingdom, it is easy for the materially well off to become what I have termed "the new marginalized."

---

22. Luke 18:18–25.

23. A capitalist eschatology in the sense of personal progression achieved through increased wealth—representative of the imbalanced economic systems of the world that for many perpetuate the divide between rich and poor.

24. Cloke and Pears, *Mission in Marginal Places*, 34.

25. Cloke and Pears, *Mission in Marginal Places*, 35.

26. Cloke and Pears, *Mission in Marginal Places*, 37.

27. Luke 19:1–10.

Chapter 4

Equipping Post-Secular Missionaries

Andrew Hardy

Introduction

In order to equip each of us to be missionaries in the post-secular city we need to be clear about the missionary nature of the Triune God. If we are to expand our evangelical focus to include not just the measured poor but also the new marginalized, then we need to ensure that we are clear about the call of Christ to work among these different groups. In what ways might we discern whom God is calling us to work among in a community at any given time if we do not hear the voice of the missionary Spirit?

David Bosch defined a primary attribute of God to be missionary.[1] Bosch's fundamental thesis was that the Father sent the Son into the world to reveal God's nature and to restore humanity's broken relationship with God. The Spirit was sent to make reconciliation with God through the work of the Son available to the whole of creation. Spiritual theologians, like myself, would argue that the Spirit's role is also to develop the spiritual intimacy of each

---

1. Bosch, *Transforming Mission*, 300–303.

believer with God. In other words, the Spirit might be claimed to enable us to have a dialogical relationship with God.

If we are to discern whom Christ is calling us to work among at any given time then we need to learn how to converse with God. This more mystical kind of spiritual theology is built on an appreciation of the Triune God as a social being. I have written about how to develop this kind of conversational relationship with God in other published works.[2] A key tenet of the Christian tradition is that the God of Jesus Christ is a personal being who reveals himself through the ongoing work of the Holy Spirit. The Father's act of sending the Son and Spirit into the world is for the purposes of reconciling humanity and the world to God.[3] The term "reconciliation" is used by Paul in 2 Corinthians 5:16–21 to describe what God suggestively seeks to achieve through Christ and his followers.

In Paul's theology, each follower of Christ is defined as an "ambassador" of God sent and empowered by the presence of the Spirit of Jesus to invite people into communion with God.[4] All peoples of the world are called to become part of God's family.[5] To be reconciled is to be brought into a right relationship as part of God's family. Those who are reconciled are from then on termed sons and daughters of God.[6]

The family of God is based on God's social and relational being.[7] God's sociality is spoken of in Scripture as the persons of the Father, Son, and Holy Spirit and the intimate relationship in the one being of God that is shared between the persons.[8] God is three persons who are one being.

---

2. Hardy and Yarnell, *Forming Multicultural Partnerships*, 236–70.

3. 2 Cor 5:16–21.

4. 2 Cor 5:16–21.

5. Rev 7.

6. Rom 8:12–14.

7. This is particularly brought to prominence in the social doctrine of the Trinity of the Eastern Orthodox tradition. See Zizioulas, *The Eucharistic Communion and the World*.

8. Zizioulas, *Being as Communion*.

The persons of the Trinity are united in a common mutuality of love and shared purpose.[9] All those who trust in and follow Christ are to be thought of as part of God's family. The question is, do the Christian communities each of us belong to see themselves as part of the Triune family? Also, what is it that makes it important for us to understand ourselves as part of this family? And, are people in our faith-communities being shaped and formed to see themselves as sent to participate in the mission of God to reconcile people into God's family?

Mission of God Consciousness

In my research with a congregation in the UK, I have been interested in finding out how the efforts of graduate leaders who have completed missional leadership programmes at my college have impacted their congregations and organizations. In the church I have been focusing on graduate leaders have been working to transform their church members to adopt a consciousness of themselves as participants in the mission of God. Part of my research has entailed interviewing ordinary members in a congregation in one city. I have listened to their accounts of their understanding of themselves, which at times includes a conscious expression of themselves as agents of reconciliation for God's kingdom. For reasons of confidentiality, I cannot name the church where I have conducted my research so I code named it Phoenix (see later). However, I do have permission to share some of the stories I have heard. In order to do this properly, I will change any details that might make it possible to identify the people concerned. In what follows I will share a few stories that are relevant to the subject of helping to integrate new followers of Christ into the society of God's family, when people come to faith based on the efforts of God's people.

---

9. Moltmann, *The Trinity and the Kingdom of God,* 129–50.

Defining the Sociality of the Body of Christ

In the Eastern Orthodox tradition, there is what theologians term the social doctrine of the Trinity.[10] This is not the place to go into technical theology, but in essence this social doctrine defines Father, Son, and Holy Spirit as engaged in a divine "dance" based on a deep inter-relationality of love, unity, and shared purposes (known as perichoresis).[11] In this particular understanding of the Triune God, the essential point is that God is not a lone, singular being but a relational, personal being. Human beings, men, women, and children, are claimed to have been made in the image of the Triune God, according to Genesis 1:26.

In other words, to be fully formed in the image of God is to live in a deep committed relationship with the Triune God and one another. The body of Christ is one body, united as a family and new society under the reign of God's love and mercy. Hence, anyone who is reconciled to God is also reconciled into the family of God.[12] We all become one body with numerous diverse gifts basing our interactions on God's love as we care for and support each other.[13]

This way of being will also include love and interaction with the people of broader society as we act as kingdom ambassadors.[14] Hence, each of us might think of ourselves as called to act as the hands and feet of Jesus to the world, giving people the message of God's love so that they too might become part of God's eternal family. This might be termed the *goal* of God's mission, that we all become part of the Father's eternal family and ambassadors for it.

I would add here that the social and spiritual capital of God's people, when they participate in God's mission, is based on the deposit of the image of the Triune God that they embody among secular peoples through their words and deeds. Moreover, their

---

10. Holmes, *Trinity in Human Community*.
11. Fiddes, *Participating in God*, 47, 48, 71–78, 81, 83, 86.
12. 1 Cor 12.
13. 1 Cor 12.
14. 2 Cor 5:16–21.

spiritual capital can be drawn on as a kind of bank account that will be accessible to people in a manner that means they draw also on the work of the Spirit at work in their relationships with believers.

Case Example

In the missional church I have been investigating, I met a couple. Dominic and Natasha shared how seeing themselves as members of their church's missional family had transformed their way of understanding what God was asking of them as a couple. They shared how in the past, before the development of the church's present missional ministry team, it had not been seen as a community that was called to equip and send out its member's as missional disciple-makers. Instead, the leaders of the church had been conceived of (at an unconscious level by members) as the professionally trained Christians, those whose role it was to look after church members. The role of church members was to come to church to receive ministry from these leaders. The role of members (during this time) was to bring friends or family to church in order to hear the gospel preached by the professional pastor at a visitors' service. The leader's role was to be the professional preacher, evangelist, and care-provider to the members. This had the effect of disempowering members, making them see themselves as supporters of the trained leader by paying tithes and offerings. They were like cheerleaders who were placed in the role, as social actors, as supporters on the sidelines of the pastor's ministry. This was not a church that saw itself as the missional body of Christ. It rather made the pastor and elders the only members of the body that really did anything of significance.

Dominic and Natasha shared how this had changed with the arrival of the new leader. The new ministry team he developed had the effect of empowering members to discover their gifts and to exercise them. Over about a nine-year period, Phoenix Church members were encouraged through teaching, preaching, church fellowship meetings, house groups, and training courses to come to view themselves as ministers and disciple-makers in their own right. A new vision of what it meant to be a follower of Jesus began to emerge, one where this couple and other members were also equipped to be able to share their faith with others. The new ministry team cast a vision of all members as a mobile part of the body of Christ.

This couple moved out of their house located in one part of the city and followed a call to live in a more deprived part of it. The goal was to use their home as a base to work from and as a place that modelled what it meant to be part of a Christian home and family to their neighbors. Their view of themselves as missional followers of Christ, called to discern and participate in Christ's ongoing mission, radicalized them. In their new vision, they considered they were following direct guidance from Christ to move to their new home in order to be Christ to the people of their new neighborhood. An important part of their mission was to take Christ into the homes of families, as well as to invite them to share in theirs as a model of God's family.

They are among others I have engaged with in research who have been equipped to see themselves in fresh ways as part of God's missional family. The church, as the body of Christ, needs missional leaders who equip members to develop this new kind of consciousness, as well as to act as their mentors to help them live it out. Dominic and Natasha have come to realize what it is to be part of the body of Christ's family and what it means to be filled with the lifeblood of his Spirit.

Background Theology

Dominic and Natasha's story is a typical example of what might happen when the people of God obtain a new consciousness of themselves as missionaries. It does not imply that people like Dominic and Natasha do not have the normal challenges of life. Indeed, when I interviewed them, they shared with me many of the struggles they faced. It was clear that doing what they believe God is calling them to do has been costly to them. In other words, they are real, normal people, like you and me. The important thing is that as part of their "new consciousness" they feel called to participate in Christ's ongoing mission. The focus of Dominic and Natasha moved from being church-centric to becoming theocentric.

Rather than seeing the church as the place where people receive ministry from the professional paid pastor, they now see their role to be to join Christ in his ongoing work in their community. They seem to have a theocentric vision of themselves as sent to participate in the mission of God. Christ may be said to continue to embody his presence through the work of his Spirit in women and men like this couple. They can act as Jesus' hands, feet, and voice to those they seek to influence. It is centered in Christ and the ongoing work of God's Spirit. It is an incarnational body that firstly embodies Christ in the Christian home among local neighbors. People like Dominic and Natasha are a representation and embodiment of the ongoing work of the Spirit of Christ.

Missional Cultural Capital

This new theocentric view of mission needs to be realized by God's people in their everyday lives. A new missional culture capital emerges when we see ourselves as missionaries and ambassadors of God. We can draw on the capital of this new consciousness to vivify our missional efforts in participation with the Spirit. It may mean our lives become increasingly based on becoming conveyors of a form of social and spiritual capital that, like a bank account, people can draw on to get to know our God.

In order for the church to move beyond seeing itself as a kind of welfare provider, or even simply as an evangelistic body sent to get new converts, it needs to equip its people with this kind of new consciousness. Believers need to see themselves in fresh ways as part of the intimate family of God. God's love is a gift-love based on putting others first.[15] It is sacrificial in nature.[16] This is what the

15. Matt 7:12.
16. Phil 2:1–9.

crucifixion of Christ models to the whole cosmos.[17] The meaning of life is for each believer to be shaped, formed, and to live their lives out based on the richness of living that love in everything they do.[18] Jesus did not call us to have quantity of life without quality of life.[19]

There is richness and abundance of life promised to humanity and to the whole of creation in the coming kingdom of God.[20] It is all based on the infinite resources of God's love and eternal nature that he has gifted to the cosmos through Jesus Christ his Son.[21] Paul declared to the Christians in Rome that with Christ God had given his people all things.[22] This is what we might call the missional cultural capital of the in-breaking reign of God. The Spirit of Christ is in the process of creating a brand new kingdom culture that will transcend everything this world has to offer.[23] We can start to model it to those around us as we make our homes and our life practices a representation of what it looks and feels like to have a relationship with a God who is love by nature.

Background Theology

Holmes has set out a vision for how Christian communities need to become a kind of therapeutic community in which people can come to wholeness.[24] This is eminently sensible, given that Jesus clearly declared that his ministry was to provide healing to those who came to him.[25] It is impossible to miss the emphasis in

---

17. Moltmann, *The Crucified God*, 206–303.
18. 1 Cor 13:1—14:1.
19. John 17:3.
20. Smith, *Desiring the Kingdom*, 155–230; Moltmann, *Theology of Hope*, 82–125.
21. See Stackhouse "Ethics and Eschatology."
22. Rom 8:32.
23. Eph 1:11–23.
24. Holmes, *Trinity in Human Community*.
25. Matt 9:12.

Luke-Acts on the ongoing ministry of the Spirit of Jesus.[26] Christ still heals people today.

Holmes talks about the need for believers to be salugenically formed as disciples.[27] He uses the term "salugenic" to describe the processes that leads to the development of Christians into Christ's likeness. The term salugenic suggests that this kind of discipleship brings a person to wholeness.[28] It does not simply involve physical wholeness, but a much deeper appreciation of inner, emotional, psychological, and spiritual wholeness.[29] The Christian community may be thought of as a sphere in which the Triune God of healing dwells. Holmes suggests that in order for people to come to wholeness of life in Christ they need to have their deepest spiritual needs and longings met.[30] This happens in the spiritual interior of each believer's being. What is needed is for God's people to have intimate communion with the living Christ who dwells in them by his Spirit.[31] In order for people to know that they are adopted into God's eternal family they need to learn how to hear God's voice. Holmes suggests this is fundamental to all deep inner healing and the coming to wholeness that people desire above everything else.[32] I have set out how people might go deeper in this more spiritual intimate manner in other published works.[33]

Sharing in the Life-blood of the Community

Paul's analogy of the body of Christ suggests no one person is sufficient to live an individual existence alone.[34] God has so ordered things that we have to learn to give and receive ministry from

26. Acts 16:6–10.
27. Holmes, *Trinity in Human Community*, 50, 103, 173.
28. Holmes, *Trinity in Human Community*, 50, 103, 173.
29. Holmes and Williams, *Becoming More Like Christ*.
30. Holmes and Williams, *Becoming More Like Christ*, 50, 103, 173.
31. Holmes and Williams, *Becoming More Like Christ*, 90, 94.
32. Holmes and Williams, *Becoming More Like Christ*, 90, 94.
33. Hardy, *Pictures of God*, 211–32.
34. 1 Cor 12.

each other in the body.[35] Each person has something to bring to the other.[36] No one person has all the spiritual gifts.[37] Each of us have something to offer to the help, care, and healing of others in the name of Christ.[38] This is what the body of Christ is to be as a Christ-shaped community.[39] It is to be a resource to bring each of us to wholeness, as the lifeblood of the Spirit flows from one to another as God exercises the spiritual gifts through each of us.[40] The church may be said to be an instrument in Christ's hands to equip believers[41] for works of local missionary service.[42]

Fivefold Ministries That Equip the Whole Body

Frost and Hirsch have argued for the importance of what are termed the fivefold ministries.[43] These ministries may need to become part of the operant theology of leadership structures in faith-communities. They argue that the aim of these ministries is to equip every believer for works of service.

Frost and Hirsch suggest that the work of apostles, prophets, evangelists, pastors, and teachers is to train each believer to engage in missional ministry. They comment:

> All these working together result in the equipping of the saints to do the work of ministry and in the maturity of the body. The whole framework of the letter to the Ephesians expects mutual recognition of these callings and a mutual accountability for their operation.[44]

35. Astin, *Body and Cell*.
36. Astin, *Body and Cell*.
37. Astin, *Body and Cell*.
38. Amess, *Healing the Body of Christ*.
39. Amess, *Healing the Body of Christ*.
40. Hicks, *Come to the Table*.
41. Smith, *Imagining the Kingdom*.
42. Eph 4:11–12. See Frost and Hirsch, *The Shaping of Things to Come*.
43. Frost and Hirsch, *The Shaping of Things to Come*.
44. Frost and Hirsch, *The Shape of Things to Come*, 170.

A criticism of their work might be that they seek to overly relate the ministries of apostles, prophets, evangelists, pastors, and teachers to contemporary leadership studies that draw on the insights of sociology. We certainly should be cautious not to allow sociology of this type to overly influence our interpretation of this important passage. Having noted this, I think their work is worthy of consideration.

What they achieve is to provide us with some insights into something of the functional roles of apostles, prophets, evangelists, pastors, and teachers. They demonstrate the importance of the fivefold ministries, understood as sociological categories, compared to contemporary organizational structures and the roles of those who operate in them. At the very least, I believe that sociology of this type might help us to think through something of the practical functions of these ministries and the benefits they might bring to our Christian communities. Here are some on my suggestions concerning how we might cautiously use something of their insights:

(a) The apostolic gift might equip and inspire teams in breaking new ground and planting new faith-communities in a strategic manner, based on the ability to think in fresh entrepreneurial ways of how to work in contextually relevant ways in diverse challenging contexts;

(b) The prophetic gift may challenge the church to take various initiatives inspired by the Holy Spirit seriously. The church might be challenged to move forward seeking to participate in what God is calling each of its people to participate in;

(c) The evangelistic gift most often aims at recruiting new people by the proclamation of the gospel. This gift might help to equip every member to effectively share their faith with others;

(d) The pastoral gift seeks to care for new people once part of the missional community—seeking to build them up in the faith, as well as to care for their deeper spiritual needs. This gift might help to equip believers to make disciples of others who then can do the same in turn;

(e) The teaching gift seeks to equip the people of God with a spiritual and theological content. It might be claimed to enhance and enrich each follower's understanding of God's revealed will. This gift also may help to ensure that the church is able to weigh up the prophetic vision gifts against the written deposit of the revelation of God—thus enabling God's people to rightly discern the prophetic gift and what it is calling the community to participate in.

All of these leadership gifts need to be bound together by a sense of loving service subject to the Lord. To serve is to serve as Christ did, which can include equipping God's people for works of service.

Conclusions

The people of God are to be called, equipped, and sent to follow Christ in his ongoing mission to bring people in society to wholeness in God's family. In order for the people of the body of Christ to be equipped for mission in post-secular society, they need to be formed in the body of Christ to become his hands, feet, and voice. Each of the fivefold ministry gifts have been potentially provided by the God of mission in order to mobilize the missional body of Christ. If we are to provide this kind of ministry to the traditional marginalized and new marginalized then we will need to understand the new marginalized, as they are missing from much evangelical social-gospel activism. Hence our attention turns to this question next.

Chapter 5

So Who Are the New Marginalized?

KEITH FOSTER

Introduction

Prior to being in (what some would term) full-time ministry (though I would argue we are all full-time workers for Christ), I spent fifteen years in Industry. Before this I had served for nine years in Her Majesty's Royal Navy as an engineer. My career in industry saw me progress from being an office-based engineer to junior, middle, then eventually into senior management. Whilst most of my time was employed within the defense industry, I also ventured into the motor trade, IT project management, and ultimately ended up (with my wife) owning and running a recruitment company. As I progressed up the career ladder, whilst the environment and people I dealt with would change, what became clear to me was that however many cars people owned, however big their homes or bank balances were, what they had in common was that they were all needy. I never met anyone who "had it all together," even those who initially would come across as doing so. In fact, such people would intrigue me to the point that I would often make it my special mission to come to know them and hopefully come to understand their subsequent needs. Managing directors, finance directors, hotel executives, operations managers, whatever their guise, all had *needs*, needs I knew only Jesus could meet.

I remember one such encounter with a senior human resources executive. This lady was professional, efficient, but equally had a reputation for being ruthless. Working in an industry that would know frequent seasons of redundancy, she had grown immune (so it seemed) to the emotion of the highs and lows of hiring and firing people. Basically, people were afraid of her, she was not someone you wanted to upset. With such folk, I would often try in some way, to find a "way in," to get to know them. It was not always easy. My early approach might simply have been a "good morning" or to offer a friendly smile. One time, I found myself in the staff room with her with no one else around, and noticed that she seemed somewhat distracted, her countenance sad and weary. On enquiry, it transpired that her mother was seriously ill (and had been for some time) and, outside of the workplace, she was the main carer. With long hours at work and no respite at home, this was taking its toll. My offer of prayer was gratefully and emotionally received. With her "floods" of tears breaking into my prayer for her situation, I had uncovered her vulnerability and need for someone to understand, to care; a vulnerability and desire that we all have.

The Measured Few

Of course, when it comes to measuring needs, organizations like The United States Census Bureau and The Office of National Statistics are experts. If it can be measured, they will measure it. Whether it is employment, the economy, or health; if it involves people, population, and community, the ONS are the people to go to. There is even some progress with regards measuring community social capital. Statistics and data around how we are getting along with our neighbors, close friendships, whether we are volunteering within our community, can be obtained. It is good to see more personable information being measured, but my experience in industry across a whole spectrum of people revealed needs that simply cannot easily be quantified. The need to feel a sense of value, purpose, to feel loved, accepted, emotionally secure, etc.; the list goes on.

What this means is that when it comes to measuring our communities, there is a whole raft of data and people that are not being considered, yet whom all have very real needs. When embarking on my doctoral research, it was this aspect of ignored need that I identified as the "gap" in research, a gap that only the one who understands and empathizes with all our needs and challenges can fill. Yet the stark reality of the situation when it comes to the urban-facing church is that often the church responds and focuses solely on the measured needs. This makes sense: to find out what the local practical needs are, to devise a project or program, and fill the gap. This is a practical and pragmatic approach and one that is needed.

The church's response to the marginalized is a clear measure of our kingdom commitment.[1] My question remains: if all have needs, what about the "new marginalized?" those whose needs are not easily identifiable, who may present more of a challenge to the church as they appear to be, and may even communicate "self-sufficiency"? The Bible tells us different. At the very heart of the Luke 18 account of Jesus and the rich young man is the fact that despite his religious adherence since childhood and his expressed desire to inherit eternal life, there was a deep sadness connected with his dependence on money and possessions. As the rich young man clung onto these things, refusing to let them go, he also clung onto his sadness. Whatever happened to that rich young man? Many such people like this surround our churches, unreached, unmeasured, and unhappy. The challenge of this book is for the urban community-facing church to expand its nets; to move beyond the comparatively "easy pickings" of the measured needy and to broaden out the conversation.

1. Matt 25:31–46.

Broadening Out the Conversation

In addition to the argument that suggests "all are needy," there are also other, important ethical considerations when it comes to serving the welfare-community demographic with an evangelical gospel intentionality: are we allowing this demographic to dominate the church's resources and attention?

Paul Cloke raises some important considerations around faith-based organizations (FBOs) mixing "service and proclamation" amongst the vulnerable. Whilst Baker's research provides significant insights into the relationship and conversational development between FBOs and their communities, the tensions created where a more overt gospel intentionality is indicated have by and large been ignored.

Cloke goes some way to addressing this tension with regards evangelical FBOs and their approach to marginalized community groups, warning of the dangers of evangelizing the vulnerable, with any subsequent spiritual demand on service-users being potentially seen as an "emotional fee."[2] Cloke's work and focus on the evangelical church's engagement with the marginalized provides helpful and insightful cautions.

In addition to raising important ethical issues with regards evangelizing the vulnerable, Cloke (as an evangelical) also sees the risk of churches and FBOs simply filling the gap of failing governments when it comes to welfare provision. Cloke states the importance of FBOs maintaining their identity, cautioning that:

> We need to be extremely careful not to assume that the locally contextualized practices of FBO welfare and caring activities merely mirror the neoliberal environment in which those contexts are set.[3]

There is a fine tension when it comes to overt gospel declaration amongst the vulnerable service-users of welfare projects. Focusing on a broader demographic of people, including non-welfare

---

2. Cloke, Beaumont, and Williams, *Working Faith*, 32.
3. Cloke, Beaumont, and Williams, *Working Faith*, 11.

projects, with an equal gospel intentionality might go some way to negating such a criticism. To date, a lot of attention has been given to how churches from all traditions might engage with the measured marginalized. Significant activity and related research into this engagement has been carried out with such initiatives as The Church Urban Fund[4] being set up in response to such reports as the 1985 *Faith in the City* report produced by the Church of England. In the absence of measured and obvious need, other felt needs are considered just as important, yet with areas of measured deprivation (economic, education, and health) often being the focus of church funding. As stated earlier, there is a danger that those outside the ONS-measured deprivation statistics can be excluded from the church's gaze too. With regards to the kingdom, it is easy for the materially well off to become the real marginalized. An additional caution is also necessary here too. It can be easy to class whole areas as "deprived" or "well-off." Estates and communities can be labelled. Yet it is important to understand that deprivation is a measure of the *people* and not a geographical area, as a recent UK local government report stated:

> A geographical area itself is not deprived: it is the circumstances and lifestyles of the people living there that affect its deprivation score. It is important to remember that not everyone living in a deprived area is deprived—and that not all deprived people live in deprived areas.[5]

This is an important consideration as it can be easy for researchers and churches alike to categorize whole geographical areas as "poor" or "middle class." An area may be classed as being deprived because it has higher-than-average levels of unemployment, educational attainment, etc. Yet this might subsequently lead churches within areas of considered higher deprivation to neglect the "new marginalized" within their communities; the new marginalized are everywhere. This raises the question of how we might work incarnationally among the new marginalized.

4. https://www.cuf.org.uk/about-us.
5. *Insight: The English Indices of Deprivation*, 2015.

Chapter 6

Grounded Theory, Methods, and Means of Embodying Jesus among the New Marginalized

Andrew Hardy

Introduction

I have based much of my ethnographic research on an adapted version of grounded theory. The important thing about grounded approaches is that they seek to begin at the point of what people want to share about their life situations. Of course, there is no such thing as a real starting point from the ground up in any research because people's lives precede any account they make of their experiences, precluding any real ground-zero starting point. However, at the very least we might say that we seek to begin with what people have to say about their present circumstances when we seek to engage in research alongside of them. It is the practical ordinary wisdom of the people of God when we engage them in research of this type that helps us to understand something of the orthopraxy of missional work among the new marginalized.

Case Example

During my research I came across the story of Sarah. Sarah shared how she spent several weeks in hospital having undergone major surgery. During this time she got to know another woman called Emily.[1] Emily, like Sarah, was recovering from treatment for cancer that had involved radical surgery. Emily fits into the category of what Keith termed the "new marginalized." As both women recovered together, they began to build up a friendship. Emily was most certainly asking important questions about life, including those related to why she was going through her illness. Sarah was careful to listen to her, and not to push her own faith-story onto Emily. During the last week of Sarah's and Emily's stay together in the ward, Sarah plucked up the courage to offer to say a nighttime prayer before the two women went to sleep. Emily said she would appreciate that.

The days that followed dragged by slowly for the two women. They often shared their frustrations of having to be limited to their life in the ward. However, like most stays in hospital, the discharge process was quite rapid. Sarah left the ward while Emily was having an X-ray. They had both agreed to keep in touch after they left hospital. It was not possible to exchange contact details before Sarah went home.

Sarah took a couple more weeks to recuperate at home and decided, during this period, to phone the ward to ask to speak to Emily if she was still there so that they could exchange contact details. The ward nurse told Sarah that Emily had been discharged. She was not able to provide her with Emily's contact details due to hospital confidentiality policy. Sarah could not remember Emily's surname. All that Sarah knew was that Emily lived in an apartment block in the same city.

Sarah recovered enough to be able to take short walks and to drive. During her convalescence, she had increasingly felt that

---

1. None of the names used in this chapter are the real names of those I include and I anonymize details so as to make it impossible to identify the participants in my research.

God wanted her to connect with Emily. What was she to do? After praying for guidance for several days, she felt that she needed to go out in her car seeking guidance from the Spirit to find Emily. She worried she had imagined this prompting, but she also wanted to be sure that she was not mistaken. Sarah shared the story of her car journey, and how she felt guided to go to a suburb of the city, then to turn into an estate, and then to park in the visitor parking of an apartment block. She felt directed to go to one of the security doors of a block of flats. She pressed one of the buttons. To her surprise she heard what sounded like Emily's voice. Emily was bowled over with surprise and invited Sarah in. Sarah shared with Emily how she had felt that God wanted her to find Emily.

She also shared how special Emily was to God. This first visit to Emily's home was among one of many that followed. Over the months, Emily came to a fuller appreciation of Christ. This is a true account. It is not the kind of story that gets reported on TV or radio documentaries. It illustrates that Christ is at work in the urban context. Sarah was enabled by the guidance of the Spirit to find Emily. The way that Sarah was guided to Emily is part of what I term the pre-ecclesial work of the Holy Spirit. In other words, Christ may be said to be at work through the Spirit among people long before they go to a church to seek the professional services of a minister.

Theological Backdrop

Long before people become part of churches the Spirit of Christ seems to be at work among them. In order for post-secular missionaries to share their spiritual capital with others, they will inevitably need to learn to be sensitive to the guidance of the Spirit like Sarah was. Her story might seem rather remarkable. The sort of thing that happened to her is only one of many ways that we might seek to discern the pre-ecclesial work of the Spirit among those we encounter in the urban context. In order to broaden the scope of mission engagement it is important for believers to learn how to cooperate with signs of the Spirit's work in other's lives.

Lesslie Newbigin spoke of the guiding work of the sovereign Spirit of God as a vital part of a Trinitarian vision of missio Dei.[2] Part of the missional disciple's DNA is the spiritual capital that is invested in each believer's life. This spiritual capital is not derived from humanistic efforts but rather it is a gift of God the Spirit. It is the Spirit that gives each of us "a spirit of revelation and inspiration in the knowledge of him."[3] The writer to the Ephesians here claims that God provides believers with the new spiritual capacity to receive revelations from God. Hence, a proper spiritual theology needs to take this teaching of Scripture seriously. It might be claimed to be of key importance as to how God's people might engage in God's mission, as they are empowered by the Spirit with the message of his Son.

Newbigin framed his theology of participation in the mission of God on an economic Trinitarian theology. He commented somewhat prophetically:

> I have affirmed that God's kingship is present in the church; but it must be insisted that it is not the property of the church. It is not domesticated within the church. Mission is not simply the self-propagation of the church by putting forth of the power that inheres in its life. To accept that picture would be to sanction an appalling distortion of mission. On the contrary, the active agent of mission is a power that rules, guides, and goes before the church: the free, sovereign, living power of the Spirit of God. Mission is not just something that the church does; it is something that is done by the Spirit, who is himself the witness, who changes both the world and the church, who always goes before the church in its missionary journal.

---

2. Newbigin, *The Open Secret,* 54.
3. Eph 1:17–19.

... From the very beginning of the New Testament, the coming of Jesus, his words and works are connected directly with the power of the Spirit.

The pre-ecclesial work of the missionary Spirit of the Triune God may be diagrammed.

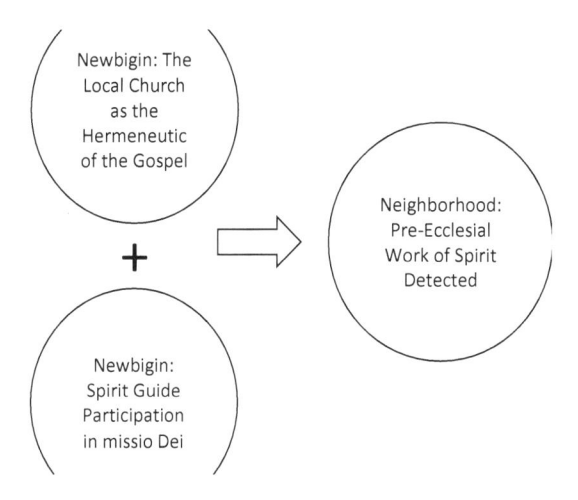

```
┌─────────────────┐
│ Newbigin: The   │
│ Local Church    │
│ as the          │
│ Hermeneutic     │
│ of the Gospel   │         ┌─────────────────┐
└─────────────────┘         │ Neighborhood:   │
                            │ Pre-Ecclesial   │
         +          ⟹       │ Work of Spirit  │
                            │ Detected        │
┌─────────────────┐         └─────────────────┘
│ Newbigin:       │
│ Spirit Guide    │
│ Participation   │
│ in missio Dei   │
└─────────────────┘
```

Each follower of Christ may seek to be equipped to discern the pre-ecclesial work of the Spirit in their daily life-contexts. Newbigin classically stated one important theological insight. He suggested that the Spirit of Christ is still active in the world today. The Spirit is suggested to enable believers to participate in the work Christ is still engaged in, in the lives of faith-seeking people.[4]

Reading Signs of the Spirit's Work— Connecting with the Life-blood

It has been suggested already that too often the church has focused much more on its efforts with the marginalized and vulnerable poor to the neglect of working with what Keith terms the "new

4. Newbigin, *The Open Secret*, 54.

marginalized." It is important to broaden the scope of missionary endeavor in the urban context to include this new marginalized category. David Bebbington's[5] and Rob Warner's[6] work demonstrates that evangelical activism and conversionism too readily focuses attention on those with the least in terms of economic capital. The question might be asked, how can we equip people to read the signs of the Spirit's work in the life-contexts of both the marginalized and new marginalized? The diagram below adds another dimension for discussion to that above.

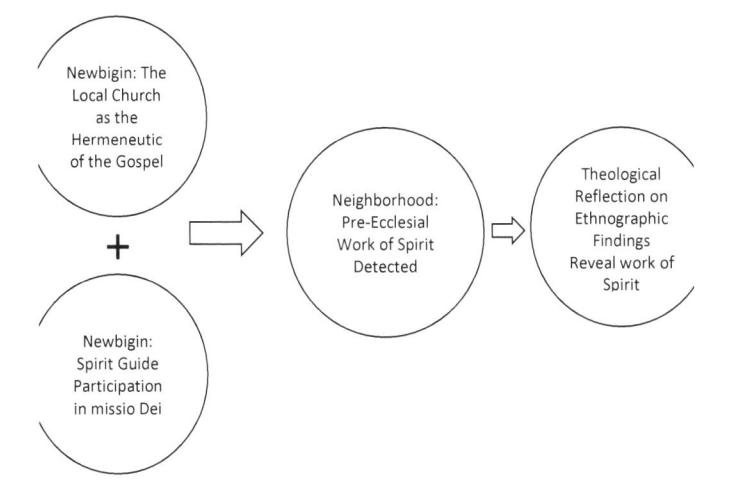

```
[Newbigin: The Local Church as the Hermeneutic of the Gospel]
         +                    →  [Neighborhood: Pre-Ecclesial Work of Spirit Detected]  ⇒  [Theological Reflection on Ethnographic Findings Reveal work of Spirit]
[Newbigin: Spirit Guide Participation in missio Dei]
```

Craig Van Gelder suggests that it is possible for ethnographic grounded research to be used in order to consider possible evidences of God's influence on people in society.[7] In order to properly evaluate whether God might be at work in someone's life, or that of a group, it is important to theologically reflect on what might be signs of the Spirit's work. For example, in the case of the story of Sarah and Emily, Sarah came to the conviction that Emily's "why questions" were a sign of the Spirit awakening her interest in discovering the meaning of her life. Sarah's theological reflections on Emily's questions and emerging interest, were further

5. Bebbington, *Evangelicalism in Modern Britain*.
6. Warner, *Reinventing English Evangelicalism 1966–2001*.
7. Van Gelder, *The Missional Church in Context*.

confirmed when Emily responded positively to the suggestion that Sarah pray for them both. Further evidence of the Spirit's guiding work was then provided by the remarkable guidance of Sarah to Emily's apartment.

At a very simple level, Sarah acted as a kind of participant observer (without being aware of it), like an ethnographer, of what she witnessed in terms of her interactions with Emily. Her theological reflections were also deeply invested with spiritual discernment of the Spirit's guiding work. Christian missional communities can use the tools of ethnography and theological reflection more intentionally and consciously than Sarah did, in order to help them to understand communities they might want to discern the Spirit's work among. In order for the body of Christ to meaningfully act as the hermeneutic of the living Christ to others, it may need to seek to embody itself in a contextually relevant manner suited to the language and culture of the groups they feel called to work among.

Contextualization begins with what is often termed social exegesis. In the diagram below a community exegesis process is detailed.

Community (Social) Exegesis

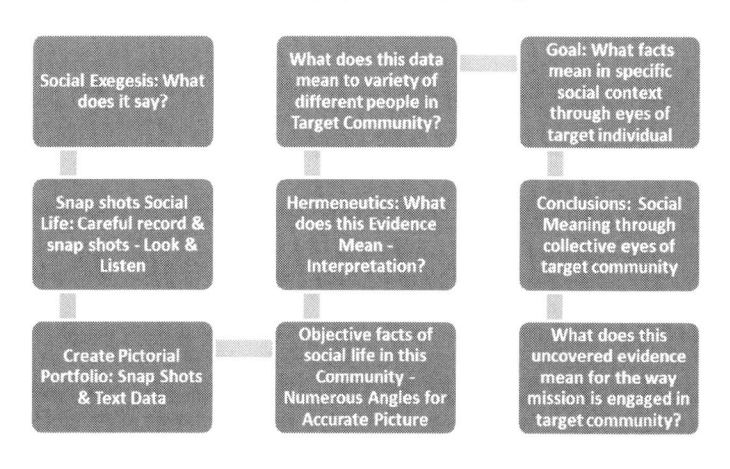

Social Exegesis: What does it say?	What does this data mean to variety of different people in Target Community?	Goal: What facts mean in specific social context through eyes of target individual
Snap shots Social Life: Careful record & snap shots - Look & Listen	Hermeneutics: What does this Evidence Mean - Interpretation?	Conclusions: Social Meaning through collective eyes of target community
Create Pictorial Portfolio: Snap Shots & Text Data	Objective facts of social life in this Community - Numerous Angles for Accurate Picture	What does this uncovered evidence mean for the way mission is engaged in target community?

Preamble: The Grounds for Exegesis

It seems important for any missional team to understand that not-yet-Christian people in the Western hemisphere are not normally attracted to churches in large numbers. They do not take part in programs designed to attract them to the sacred space of the church building.[8]

The 2009 American Religious Identification Survey,[9] provides an interesting picture of what might help to identify the so-called "cultural memory of Christianity" in the United States of America. It does not as such provide a cultural analysis of national memory. However, in my view, it does provide important data regarding the beliefs of people in the US postmodern cultural context. For example, in Table 4 on page 8 of the survey a consideration of "Beliefs about God among the U.S. adult population regarding the existence of God" is analyzed. Only 2.3 percent said there is no such thing as God. 4.3 percent said there is no way to know if God exists. 5.7 percent were not sure. 12.1 percent said they believed in a higher power but not in a personal God. 69.5 percent were definite in their belief in a personal God. 6.1 percent refused to give an opinion. What this data reveals is that at least 24.4 percent of the US population do not have a Christian faith as such, although it is important to be cautious about making this claim based on the data found in this survey.

However, Jon Meacham, in an article published in *Newsweek* on Saturday 2nd March 2019, makes this important observation based on an interview he had with Albert Mohler Jr., president of the Southern Baptist Theological Seminary. In it, Mohler shares his concerns about the changes in the American Christian religious culture:

> The central news of the survey was troubling enough [to Mohler]: the number of Americans who claim no religious affiliation has nearly doubled since 1990, rising

---

8. Frost and Hirsch, *The Shape of Things to Come*, chapters 1–3.

9 American Religious Identification Survey [ARIS 2008]. Summary Report March 2009. Barry A. Kosmin and Ariela Keysar.

Body and Blood

from 8 to 15 percent. Then came the point he could not get out of his mind: while the unaffiliated have historically been concentrated in the Pacific Northwest, the report said, "this pattern has now changed, and the Northeast emerged in 2008 as the new stronghold of the religiously unidentified." As Mohler saw it, the historic foundation of America's religious culture was cracking.

"That really hit me hard," he told me last week. "The Northwest was never as religious, never as congregationalized, as the Northeast, which was the foundation, the home base, of American religion. To lose New England struck me as momentous." Turning the report over in his mind, Mohler posted a despairing online column on the eve of Holy Week lamenting the decline—and, by implication, the imminent fall—of an America shaped and suffused by Christianity. "A remarkable culture-shift has taken place around us," Mohler wrote. "The most basic contours of American culture have been radically altered. The so-called Judeo-Christian consensus of the last millennium has given way to a post-modern, post-Christian, post-Western cultural crisis which threatens the very heart of our culture." When Mohler and I spoke in the days after he wrote this, he had grown even gloomier. "Clearly, there is a new narrative, a post-Christian narrative, that is animating large portions of this society," he said from his office on campus in Louisville, KY."

Mohler's reflections on the 2009 American Religious Identification Survey express concern on the changes in the Christian religious culture of North America. It is well worth taking this survey into consideration, as it demonstrates the increasing cultural shifts occurring in North America that bespeak a decreasing memory of life informed by a so-called "Christian cultural memory." It may well be that the US is behind the trend of a 40 percent loss of Christian memory in the UK, but it is vital to take into account the need for Christian mission to extend to mission in third places. It is likely that it will become increasingly important in the US context, for Christian mission to be informed by a sacramental theology, that places each believer as a disciple-maker sent out by the Triune God to participate in the missio Dei in third places. We are finding this to be true in the UK context increasingly. It is our argument that we need to strategize about working with a new marginalized, who are arguably increasingly being marginalized because of the loss of a Christian memory. This loss of Christian memory is obviously different to a new marginalized, who are marginalized by the evangelical tradition because they are wealthy instead of being part of the preferred poor.

As mentioned above, at least 40 percent of people have no cultural memory of Christianity in the UK.[10] Many of them probably have no meaningful relationships with Christians. Therefore, there is little chance they will be attracted to Christian people and inherited forms of church. Church life is an alien sub-culture to them. Rather missional teams will need to embed in communities with which they have a good cultural fit. They will need to build relationships with not-yet-Christians for quite some time before any impact occurs. Over the years a target community needs to have a chance to meet Christ through the Christians who incarnationally live among them. Mission in the West would seem to need to engage in pre-gospel evangelism (i.e., Does God exist? Is there meaning to life? etc.), based on building meaningful and genuine relationships with people.

The goal will not be to get faith-seekers to embrace the churches from which these teams originate. The strategy formulated may be better conceived as seeking to share the absolutes of the gospel with faith-seekers and to let them apply them by the guidance of the Spirit suited to their context. This probably means we will not see new churches planted so often if we adopt this approach. Culturally relevant expressions of what it means for people to focus on Christ will take negotiation between how their culture expresses awe and wonder and how Scripture might help them to be informed of what is at the heart of Christian views of God. This sets a new paradigm for mission. We would seem to need to experiment with new ways of shaping the lives of people

---

10. Stoddard and Cuthbert, *Church on the Edge*, 30.

whom Christians seek to influence in their neighborhoods. Ordinary Christians, you and I, will need to act like guides at the side helping new believers to make sense of their newfound faith suited to the immediate concerns of their context. Fresh expressions[11] of these types of missional communities probably will need to be allowed to re-invent church to become what it once was—authentic community that is developed by converts suited to their sub-culture (i.e., specific ways of life). This kind of approach will make it important to engage in proper research concerning the communities to be engaged in mission. Let us consider social exegesis as a step-by-step process which hopefully will enable us to better understand communities we want to work within.

Case Example

The case example below is based on a study of a local mission team's search to understand a village community that they wished to work among. Their team took three main steps in going about their social study. They did this by making observations of people and places in the village community. They recorded findings in research diaries and sought feedback from community members of their views of their community. Consider the steps they took:

Step 1: A first step in seeking to understand the people in a local neighborhood and their outlooks on it, is to seek to capture the views of people who live there about the things of importance to them. This is done by determining what social behavior reveals about a target community. A team member commented:

> Observation A: "We conducted a social survey of our community. This is what we observed":
>
> (a) "There was no community center utilized in the village for young people to get to know each other to socialize in";

---

11. Moynagh and Harrold, *Church for Every Context*.

(b) "There were some extended family networks[12] of inter-related families that provided some social cohesion to youth in some families, but mostly there were only nuclear families that lacked this provision";[13]

(c) "Some social gatherings occurred among mothers when picking children up from primary school";

(d) "There was a mother and toddler group where mothers got together";

(e) "The pub had a small selection of local patrons as regulars but there was nothing for young people";

(f) "A large playground was an arena for children to play in after school. It was a meeting place for youth in the evenings most nights during the summer months";

(g) "A drama club put on seasonal small productions in a village hall, but youth were not involved in this group";

(h) "Teenagers met each morning in numbers of about fifty to catch a local bus to take them to school";

(i) "Some very limited socializing took place among friendly nuclear family groups and youth did not as such take part in these limited get-togethers";

(j) "Mostly nuclear families did not socialize together except for Christmas parties among neighbors in organized neighborhood watch areas,[14] but youth did not go to these as such either";

(k) "The local Anglican church had a small congregation of mostly elderly people with no young people";

(l) "There were no local shops where young people could meet."

12. An extended family consists of more than just mother, father, and children as a single autonomous group, uncles, aunts, grandparents live more closely with each other, often sharing life together as a community

13. This is a single family unit made up of mother, father, and children unrelated with close family ties as in an extended family.

14. Neighborhood watch is a scheme where people in a community work together to be vigilant for local crime that can be reported to local law enforcement to help reduce crime in a neighborhood.

They then gathered photographs as snapshots representative of the above observations and put them in a portfolio. They added captions to the pictures and paraphrased comments of what they might mean. A key question was, what are the challenges that young people face in this village? Another team member commented:

> Observations B: "We listened carefully for comments that seemed to sum up the mood and needs of the various groups we identified. We gathered data from what we heard from parents and youth we spoke to from time to time. We wrote these near each of the snapshots in the portfolio, for example":
>
> (a) "We noticed that a number of parents complained: 'There is no youth club.' 'The young people are damaging the children's playground.'"
>
> (b) "We noticed that some mother's complained: 'We need a nursery in the village.' 'It is too far to . . . take our kids to . . . .'"

Step 2: (Hermeneutics) What Does This Data Mean to the Target Community?

Because of this team's background in youth mission they decided to focus on "Observation A." They took some time collecting more photographic snapshots. They obtained more comments from parents. They also sought to identify other places young people met. They then took their portfolio to show to young people in the community, seeking their interpretations of the pictures and recorded the comments they obtained from this feedback. They also conducted video interviews with them. They promised that they would let them see their video-recorded interviews at the local village hall one evening with some arranged games and snacks, etc. Feedback demonstrated a number of collectively held views shared by the youth. All were recorded in the portfolio for later reference. Some of the comments included:

(a) That it would be good to have a comfortable place to meet;

(b) That youth didn't want to be told what to do, but a youth group with various games equipment and some organized social events would be welcome;

(c) That having someone to speak to confidentially about life problems would be welcome.

Collective Interpretation

This mission team decided to put a summary of the interviews together as a short video-documentary seeking to express the views of the young people. They also added some interpretations and suggestions of what was communicated to them by the youth in this video. They concluded this short documentary with questions for small groups to discuss after the viewing at the village hall. Young people were invited to the viewing at the venue. Small groups reported back responses and ideas to questions that led to a shared view that they wanted a youth group to meet in the village hall. The team thanked the young people for coming and promised to arrange another meeting a few weeks later to see what could be done.

Step 3: What Did This Evidence Mean for the Way This Team Might Go About Their Mission with the Young People?

Prayer was obviously part of their search for meaning, seeking God's guidance for how they should respond to the views they had discovered. After a few meetings together they decided to meet again with the young people. They reached the conclusion that they needed to offer a youth group that would have a social component, games area, tuck shop, and an informal means for young people to chat with team members for pastoral support. The team recognized that the youth also wanted to take some responsibility for their club as well. It was agreed with them that they would get involved in seeking permission from the village hall caretaker to obtain use of the venue with the youth team being responsible overall for the facility and club activities. A four-month pilot scheme was agreed upon to see how things proceeded.

Analysis of Findings

What this process illustrates, in a sound-bite fashion, is a condensed version of a social exegesis of a target community. Through this process, the hope was to build relationships with young people in the community. It was determined that there was a good fit of the missional youth team concerned to be able to work with the local village's youth sub-culture. This finding was confirmed to a large extent by the young people's willingness to engage in positive dialogue with the team. This seemed like a good fit to proceed to suggesting a pilot process for a youth mission in this village.

This was all conceived as a possible way ahead for a longer term pre-evangelism process among them. Another lesson was that in the missional suburban context straightforward gospel communication would not be the strategy utilized to reach out to these young people. Instead *pre*-evangelism would need to address prior questions like, does God exist? None of this could be done in a programmatic manner, but rather would need to arise when interest was evident to explore matters like this. These kinds of questions came out quite naturally from the young people even during the time of conducting the social exegesis. Hence, it seemed natural that they might from time to time in the future raise them in conversations.

In the case of planning for this project the team had not hidden their faith, but neither did they push it. There was a desire to be transparent. The team was intentionally made up of practicing Christians with a desire to serve the local youth community and its families. A fundamental conviction of the team was that it was seeking to connect with opportunities the Spirit might provide to participate in mission with these young people. A key goal was to embody Christ to these youth through the lives of the team. In one sense, learning about the lifeblood of the youth community and their families was a way of connecting with the lifeblood of the Spirit of Christ potentially at work among them. The team was careful to take note of the questions the youth asked or the issues they faced. They were mindful that possible signs of the Spirit's work might be evident in what was said or at times done by the young people. The team also sought to obtain the local Anglican church's permission to act as a moderator of the team's work among the young people. The local vicar was more than willing to sit on some of their meetings to provide spiritual oversight. There were also important child protection and vulnerable person's guidelines to be observed. The team ensured it went through all the proper legislated checks to obtain clearance to work with the youth. The local vicar would act as their child protection officer.

Serving an Apprenticeship among New Expressions of the Emerging Body of Christ

As a Christian minister, educator, and researcher I have had the very real privilege of working among a wide range of people of all ages. A key conviction that I have always sought to maintain is the need for me to keep on learning. One way this has worked out is that I seek, every year, to act in some kind of learning context where I do not lead, but rather learn from those around me. This has partly arisen from my commitments in missiology and ethnographic participant research. We never come to a point where we can call ourselves experts. In fact "experts" have often led to the church relying on them instead of seeking to discern and to follow the pre-ecclesial work of the Spirit. We are always called to continuous humility and learning. John the Baptist once said, speaking of Jesus, "He must increase but I must decrease."[15] This ancient saying has informed the posture of my heart.

---

15. John 3:30.

Body and Blood

I believe that each of us are called to humble intelligent service seeking to follow what Christ is doing in each new context we engage in. In the last few years I returned to one of the fundamental areas of my work in Christian ministry—youth work. I could not fulfill a role in a church, but rather I went as a helper with leaders of five youth groups to Soul Survivor, a large Christian annual youth event. As I spent time alongside the young people, of what sociologists now term generation Z (eight to twenty-one year old's), I was interested to serve a kind of apprenticeship among them, learning from them about their challenges and faith questions.[16] This apprenticeship also involved seeking to be apprenticed by observing for signs of the Spirit's work by the young people's questions and interests so that I might learn how the Spirit might guide my work with them.

The point I want to make here is that in order for us to appropriately contextualize the Christian story to the lives of those we are called to work among, we need to be ready to serve a kind of apprenticeship with them. They need to teach us how to relate to them in relevant ways. It is important that when we seek to share our faith with others we do so making it obvious that we are Christians. We may seek to follow the Good Shepherd's leading. We play follow my leader. It will be important to help them understand that the motivation for change in their lives is based on the real influence of a personal God at work within them.

This is quite a different approach to missional discipleship than was the case in years past. It dethrones would-be expert Christians who are motivated by their own agendas, often seeking for affirmation because people look to them for the answers. I suggest that we have no answers, except that we take the posture, "he must increase and I must decrease." Only by following evidences of the Spirit at work ahead of us in faith-seekers' lives can we really be effective as participants in the Triune mission. We need to actually trust that the Spirit of Christ works in fresh new ways in people's lives before we get to be part of their journeys. If we are to meaningfully become part of what Christ is doing among them,

---

16. Hardy and Yarnell, *Missional Discipleship After Christendom*, 171–95.

then we need to follow the work of his Spirit in their lives, looking for evidence of what the Spirit of Jesus is inspiring in them. How does your missional community form its strategies for mission among those it feels called to work among? How might radical deconstruction of your approach look if what we seek to discern is the Spirit at work ahead of us?

Imagining New Forms for Expressing a Christ-Like Culture

My experience with the youth of generation Z at several Soul Survivor events over the last few years helped me to track with changes in youth culture. Pete Ward has done much to highlight the ongoing significance of worship music as a means of conveying the gospel story to these generations.[17] In *Participation and Mediation*, he has offered a critical voice to a consumerist, market-driven worship-music industry. He argues that it can have the effect of leading young people to make Christian worship experience the most important part of what it means to be a follower of Christ. The effect of this is that it creates the appearance that Christian life needs to be based on spiritual highs, produced by worship experiences, instead of seeking a more balanced outlook where every aspect of human life is important, including the hard and messy parts of it. His main point is that a shallow gospel that responds to the current niche-market consumerist worship music economy has tended to reduce interest in developing deeper, more mature followers of Christ. He concedes, nevertheless, that contemporary branded forms of worship music have witnessed genuine life-changing conversions among young people. He suggests that young people learn from it, but he also recognizes that other approaches need to be used in addition to it to bring them to lifelong, lasting commitment and change.

It also seems warranted to recognize that much of young people's espoused and operant theology come to awareness through

---

17. Ward, *Participation and Mediation*, 7, 9, 13, 23, 24, 27, 118, 156.

the inherent normative theology in many worship songs. All of this might be claimed to be part of one way that a fresh approach to cultivating and expressing a spiritual cultural capital might help young people to become like Christ. Ward's critique of consumerist worship culture also recognizes that God does seem to work through it as well.[18] It often seems to create a desire for the latest experience to be obtained in the newest songs and Christian events where they are performed.[19] As a result, an experience that makes young people feel good can detract from the demands of the gospel of Christ for some hardship, genuine repentance, and sacrifice.[20]

In other words, a consumerist ideology may have created a culture where good experiences are valued as they are consumed in the latest worship events and the products these events promote for purchase and consumption. It can fail to more deeply and intentionally shape disciples who will commit to follow Christ in the hard times.

Having said this, I was very impressed with the young people whom I worked with at several Soul Survivor events. They were eager to learn as much as they could about the Bible, overcoming sin and temptation, and how to become better followers of Christ in order to share their faith with their peers.

This more grounded research among them convinced me that critiques of events that, like Soul Survivor, use products and consumerism to contextualize the gospel to youth are not to be taken too far. The youth of generation Z whom I was connecting with were looking not simply for a spiritual high, but also real help to learn how to deal with the challenges of their lives.[21]

18. Ward, *Participation and Mediation*, 33–92.
19. Hardy and Yarnell, *Missional Discipleship After Christendom*, 171–95.
20. Ward, *Participation and Mediation*, 7, 9, 13, 23, 24, 27, 118, 156.

21. In my other published work, I discuss the differences that seem to characterize generation Z compared to Generation Y. Hardy and Yarnell, *Missional Discipleship After Christendom*, 171–95. We would do well to consider how to help cultivate a discipleship-formation culture that will meaningfully help youth in the urban context to explore their spiritual questions. Hardy, Whitehouse, and Yarnell, *Power and the Powers*, 56–74.

Finding the People of Peace

In Luke 10:1–12, the sending out of the seventy (or seventy-two) disciples is recounted. It is interesting that the focus of this mission passage relates *how* the seventy disciples were sent out. It was for them to seek to engage with those they discerned to be open to receive the message of the in-breaking reign of God. It required them to locate people of peace in communities they were sent to serve. The sign of peace these disciples used to identify people of peace was to look for opportunities to meaningfully interact with the key gatekeepers of these communities. In the village communities throughout Galilee were the representative elders and head families. It was most often a head man of a community who acted as a kind of gatekeeper who would vet visitors to these communities. It was vital for the disciples to be open and honest about their goals for going to such a community. It was for them to seek permission to engage in mission there. "A son of peace" would be a community gatekeeper who welcomed those sent by Christ. The sign of openness and readiness to receive the gospel of the kingdom was that those sent would be welcomed, helped, and not hindered.

Another important point to raise is that the gospel of the kingdom was intended to be good news.[22] It would be bad news if the disciples were met with hostility rather than bringing peace to a community. It would lead to conflict and hardening of opinion against the God who had sent them. In the context of present-day mission among the new marginalized, the principle follows that the optimum approach to sharing the good news of Jesus Christ with people needs to be undertaken in the context of permission-giving. Peaceful approaches need be used to promote peace with God wherever that is possible. Hostility will inevitably also arise, but this does not require that we seek to create unnecessary tensions in communities. The Beatitudes of Matthew chapter 5 remind us that the peacemakers are the authentic sons and daughters of God.

---

22. Beasley-Murray, *Jesus and the Kingdom of God*, 71–107.

Conclusions

We have considered some positive ideas that can be tried to help us understand, interact with, and work among the new marginalized in our urban and suburban contexts. In order to do this effectively we must intentionally seek to understand the contexts of those God guides us to interact with. It will not be enough that we feel called without there being corresponding evidence that people of peace, among those we feel called to, actually welcome us to engage with them. It would seem that a key principle of embodying Christ to those we share life among is that we seek to do so based on good relationships, rather than our presence being the cause of unnecessary tension and conflict.

One of the signs of the in-breaking reign of God is that its goal is to bring about the state of shalom for those who embrace the Lord.[23] The Hebrew term "shalom" means much more than peace. It means a transformation of the state of affairs in society where people seek to live in trust, love, harmony, and acceptance, seeking unity as they each live out their diverse giftedness together.[24] Shalom means a state of rest and an end to conflict. It will necessarily need to be based on intentional behaviors of peace-making and peace-keeping in the presence of the God of peace. When the eschatological kingdom is finally established it will be a kingdom of peace.

We are not called to be less than peacemakers. We are rather sent as ambassadors to reconcile men and women to peace with the Triune God. To be a messianic community that effectively incarnates Christ in amongst peoples of a community we need to embody Christ to those people. We will need to model peaceful behaviors. Incarnational mission within any community means that we join with the Spirit of the God of all places and spaces. In the next chapter we turn our intention to the importance of place.

---

23. Ott, Strauss, and Tennent, *Encountering Theology of Mission*, 130.
24. Sheldrake, *The Spiritual City*; Hill, *Signs of Hope in the City*.

Chapter 7

The Importance of Place in Community

KEITH FOSTER

The Theology of Place

God loves place. The Bible starts with God creating, not only the heavens and the earth (as overwhelmingly awesome as that is) but more specifically, a place for mankind to dwell, to procreate, to enjoy the created order, and to be with and know their Creator. Following what theologians call "the fall" (Gen 3), where our relationship with God was broken and marred by humanity's rebellion, the subsequent restoration of the relationship between God and humans, again initiated by the Creator, is covenanted, is promised, around a specific place, land, terra firma.

> The LORD had said to Abram, "Go from your country, your people and your father's household to the land I will show you. I will make you into a great nation, and I will bless you; I will make your name great, and you will be a blessing. I will bless those who bless you, and whoever

curses you I will curse; and all peoples on earth will be blessed through you."[1]

The work of Walter Brueggemann is worth reading for its full and rich treatment of the theme of "land," but it will suffice for our current considerations to acknowledge that it will be through blessed *place* and *people* that God will work out his redemptive history. Whilst humankind made in his image will be the focus and benefactors, this will all be achieved *in the context of place.*

As we travel with the people of God through Scripture on their redemptive journey, place provides the redemptive setting. Yet whilst these places vary in guise and construct (be it a mountain, tent, temple, or place of nativity), the central focus of the journey is always *towards God*. God's promise to Moses was that once rescued out of Egypt, the people would come "and worship me on this mountain."[2] The centerpiece of tabernacle and temple was not the furniture but the very presence of the Holy One of Israel. The journey of the magi ended in Bethlehem, the place where they could declare, "we . . . have come to worship him."[3]

Leonard Hjalmarson suggests that the God of redemptive history and mission "is infatuated with place,"[4] pointing to the incarnation, God with us, as the ultimate expression of this. According to Hjalmarson, the incarnation demonstrates the extent of God's commitment to place.[5] I understand this emphasis, though would offer the balance that God's ultimate focus is *people*, us, you and me. This said, God's commitment to "get dirty," to "get in the mix" in our fallen place shows the necessity of context. Humanity's relationship with the God who first loved them must be grounded in earthy, practical places. Jesus has modelled (with the

---

1. Gen 12:1–3.
2. Exod 3:12.
3. Matt 2:1.
4. Hjalmarson, *No Place Like Home,* 26.
5. Hjalmarson, *No Place Like Home,* 26.

incarnation) what is to be our approach as those commissioned to carry on with his kingdom project.[6]

This may sound obvious, but church history has shown that it can be easy for God's people to attempt to create a "spiritual other," a sacred space away from the mess and brokenness, a walled-garden, in our attempt to develop and experience a taste of "kingdom come." The various extreme monastic attempts at this have only revealed the futility of such separation.

In his high priestly prayer, speaking to the Father, Jesus made it clear, "My prayer is not that you will take them out of the world but that you protect them in it."[7] Incarnation into place, however messy, is God's modelled way. Remaining within our comfortable "walled garden" as a sole strategy cannot reproduce this, even if the title of our program has "messy" in it.

Evangelical community church buildings have been developed that exist to be a resource for unchurched people to use for activities, with the hope that these people will then come to the Christian worship services held within them. This is a strategy that has some real success. For example, one community church known to me realized considerable growth in attendance at its worship services when local unchurched people used it facilities. However, it is important that community churches take on a missional focus that encourages its members to act as missionaries in third places that are not located in places owned by the church as well. If they do not then it is likely that church members will not as such be shaped and formed to become missionaries in their work places and neighborhoods. It is the argument of this book that they need to be if we are to make a missional impact in third places like this.

My time as a pastor in a local West Midlands evangelical church in the UK has seen a transition from an attractional model of church (where everything happens in the building) to one that sees the need to incarnate, get messy, get in the mix of the local community. This was not simply an emotional decision, but one borne out of deep theological reflection on what it means to be the

6. Matt 28:19–20.
7. John 17:15.

church. Over the past ten years, theological wrestling with such questions around the nature of our Trinitarian God of mission, and how this might subsequently influence and shape our missiology, ultimately impacting the shape of our ecclesiology (how we do church), has been significant.

Creating Good and Great Places

This all said, there is an unseen enemy of the "local community place." Globalization and capitalist strategies are devouring and destroying the "forest" of local place at a rapid pace. This is not solely a church or faith-community issue; this affects everyone. It is something everyone can see and is talking about, yet something everyone feels powerless to reverse. The loss of the corner shop, the uniqueness of our city centers, all gradually being lost to multinational corporations.

One city center resembles another. Of course, these huge corporations would announce the introduction of new places; the global village, the online community, chat rooms. Are not these places too? Yes, of course, but Hjalmarson (quoting Jerry Mander) sums the situation up nicely:

> Place separated from the people who inhabit it becomes a mere fact, a calculation in a formula, subject to the application of power in the interest of profit. We pursue abstractions: removing what is personal and unique from the equation. What we fail to see is that when we franchise fast-food, we abstract humanity itself.[8]

Ray Oldenburg is a significant contributor to this whole conversation. His landmark work, *The Great Good Place* (1999), analyses the demise of place across the world. To counter this, Oldenburg considers the English Pub, the French café, the American Tavern, and the Classic Coffeehouses as third places. Third places away from our homes (first places) and places of work (second places) that historically have provided places for enhanced community

8. Hjalmarson, *No Place Like Home*, 27.

interaction. According to Oldenburg, whatever their guise, "the eternal sameness of the third place overshadows the variations in its outward appearance."[9] Oldenburg cites the uniqueness of third places and their capacity to help a community thrive. While the opportunity to "escape" to the local pub or café may be obvious, according to Oldenburg (as a social scientist), third places offer much more.[10] The neutral ground, where customers can "come and go" as they please with no hosting responsibilities. Generally, it is a place where all hierarchies (aside from the necessary proprietor and staff, whose role is to serve and create the welcome) disappear; thus, secondly, the third place is a great leveler. Places where hats and coats can be removed, discussions started, opinions expressed, an oasis of interaction. The third place is thus, and mainly, a place of conversation, with regulars and familiar menus and orders creating a home away from home.

So, is this always the experience in our coffeehouses and other third places? Sadly, it is not only fast food that has been franchised. Franchised public houses and coffee houses are also appearing and threatening the community "forest."

John Manzo, an associate professor of sociology at the University of Calgary, Canada, has produced some insightful and helpful research into what he calls third-wave coffeehouses. He not only considers the interactions of the people, but also the role of machinery and coffeehouse equipment in such places.[11] Manzo's research does not make encouraging reading. If our loved and local community third places are replaced by franchised places whose primary goal is *profit*, not people (though they of course recognize customer service is important), then the reducing grazing land for encouraging meaningful community conversation is even more at risk. Third places are an endangered species if they

---

9. Oldenburg, *The Great Good Place*, 20.

10. Oldenburg, *The Great Good Place*, 20–42.

11. Manzo, *Machines, People and Social Interaction in Third Wave Coffeehouses*.

are to be replaced by those that, according to Manzo, create "inauthentic social experiences."[12]

So, what is the answer? How might the urban community-facing church respond to such demise of the third place? The church is renowned for identifying and responding to felt needs. The emergence of food banks, clothing banks, debt counselling places are all responses to measured and discovered needs. The disappearance of third places of our community conversational grazing land is an unmeasured need that the church is well positioned to address. Considering our earlier chapters detailing the new openness of communities to embrace faith-based organizations in the community conversation (Baker's progressive localism) this could be an ideal opportunity for the re-emergence of third places within our communities. Yet, remembering our earlier caution, not simply third places for the sake of community enhancement (as honorable as that is) but third places that possess a gospel intentionality are required. Places that point to a better, grander, kingdom place with a supreme and loving Proprietor who welcomes all who would come to him.

---

12. Manzo, *Machines, People and Social Interaction in Third Wave Coffeehouses*, 1.

Chapter 8

Shaping New Sacred Places in a Post-Secular Atmosphere

Andrew Hardy

Introduction

In this chapter we will focus on the importance of shaping new sacred places in urban contexts. These sacred places might all be termed the property of the sovereign God of mission. Hence, every place is destined to come under the complete Lordship of Christ. The creation of new sacred gathering places in a community will require that the people of God intentionally seek to incarnate in secular and post-secular places alike. People seem to still seek after places of peace or safe places in which they can relax. The concept of the "sacred" has from the earliest times included a numinous quality of peacefulness. These sacred spaces will need to be given sharpness of focus through "gospel intentionality" if they are to put the living presence of Christ at their heart.

But it will only be Christ's real presence that will bring people to peace within these kinds of places. Places inhabited by a sense of the divine presence are most often places that have regularly had spiritual practices of prayer and worship take place within them. I will suggest that it is these kinds of places that might be termed "thin places" and "new storied places" where God can be encountered through conversations with the patrons of these places. (Sacred does not mean a church building. It could be a club, pub, coffee shop, or gym.)

There are four main things to concentrate our attention on in this chapter. Firstly, we need to understand the importance of "thin places" and how these remain relevant, especially in a spiritually questing post-secular Western context. Then, we will move on to a consideration of the need to develop new "storied places"[1] in the neighborhoods of those we seek to work among in mission. Following this we will consider spiritual practices that might help post-secular faith-seekers to connect with God. Finally, we will look into the importance of hospitality and generosity as the primary qualities required for missional engagement with peoples in thin places and storied places.

Thin Places

First the pagan Celts, and much later Christianized Celtic peoples, used the term "thin" to represent mesmerizing places that had the existential impact of making heaven seem close to earth. The Celtic phrase "Caol Ait" has the meaning of "thin place," or a place of intersection between heaven and earth. "Caol" means "thin" and "Ait" means "pleasant, strange, or unusual." In this sense, a "Caol Ait" was a kind of thin (translucent) location that had a sense of a strange or unusual divine presence that seemed just below the surface and approaching visibility in the material realm. It was a place discerned to be inhabited by the divine aura. It was experienced as a place of pleasant, and at times disturbing communion, with the divine. The meaning of Caol also has other ancient etymological linguistic links, including "to be stretched thin." Like a stretched

---

1. A storied place is a location invested with memories and stories of the most important things to the lives of those who inhabit these places.

membrane it would cause it to become somewhat transparent. Thin places were transparent enough to capture something of God's almost visible presence.

The well-known Celtic style of crosses (as below) have woven interconnected patterns in them. These patterns represent something of what it means for the thinness and transparency of spiritual connectivity in places where interconnection between God, and those who seek God, occur and are woven into the fabric of everyday life. Thin places were particularly important to the Celtic and Gaelic peoples and were to often be found in places of outstanding natural atmospheric beauty.[2]

However, thin places are well known to this day, to at least a few seekers, even if the names of these places do not etymologically link to the phrase "Caol Ait." In ancient times, Celtic Christians dwelt on the windswept isle of Iona or the craggy peaks of Croagh Patrick, among other places. There they obtained a sense of separation from the normal frenetic rounds of human society. Through their isolation in the rugged natural beauty of these environments, they were able to develop a deep sense of God's awesome presence among them. A modern Celtic saying is, "Heaven and earth are only three feet apart, but in thin places that distance

2. Picture taken by author of chapter of a silver Celtic cross.

is even shorter."[3] In other words, a thin place represented the close proximity of heaven to earth. A healthy Christian mystical experience of encounter with the divine matured in these so-called Caol Ait locations.

The origins of the word "thin" also goes back to old English and Germanic roots. Etymologically "thin" may be defined as "Loose or sparse," hence "easily seen through,"[4] which is clearly related to potential meanings of Caol Ait. The renascence of interest during the past twenty years in ancient Celtic Christian spirituality has drawn on the existential quality of thin places as locations in the earthly dimension that still provide a closer sense of God's presence.

Hence, the derivative notion of places that can be "easily seen through" are those settings where God seems especially close to creation and to people. The reader may know of such places. In the previous chapter Keith discussed the importance of place as nodal points where God and his people meet. It is not in some ethereal realm of spiritual transcendence that God interacts with his creation as such. The incarnation of Christ, in the space-time world of place, implies that God reveals himself in the places where people live.

Thin places may begin in the popular imagination of those to whom God reveals himself, as specific locations where this first occurred for them. In the ancient Christian Celtic context this was in places like the Isle of Iona. In the contemporary missional context of the West, new thin places might become parkland or woodland of outstanding natural beauty, where people feel in some sense close to the ground of all being and life. Indeed, I have friends who are not Christians who comment that they feel closest to "god" in these kinds of places. They might include local parks or country estates, such as those managed by National Trust in the UK or at retreat centers. It could be for younger people through music that the meanings of words get linked to the passions of their hearts, creating a thin connection between God and them. Pete Ward's

3. http://www.explorefaith.org/mystery/mysteryThinPlaces.html.
4. https://www.etymonline.com/word/thin.

early and later work clearly indicates this kind of thin quality, although he does not use the language of "thin."[5]

In biblical terms, people like John the Baptist dwelt in wilderness locations as the ancient prophets had prior to him in order to commune with God.[6] During Christ's temptation in the wilderness, he there engaged in spiritual power-encounters with the forces of evil.[7] He, there, committed himself to the mission of God for his three-year ministry prior to his crucifixion and resurrection. It is said that angels also ministered to him.[8] Jesus took his disciples with him, at times, to lonely places to find rest to reflect and to encounter God afresh.[9] Jesus spent whole nights in prayer on hillsides or craggy peaks to pray and commune with his Father.[10] Retreat, or communion with God, was arguably experienced in thin places as part of early Christian spirituality. A thin place might be defined in this sense as a place free from distractions, which facilitates an atmosphere where we can seek communion with God.

The terminology of "thin place" is not used in the Bible, but there is evidence of the practice of communing with God in places free from the hubbub of normal everyday human society.[11] For these reasons, we might at the very least accept that ancient Celtic Christians, like Christ and his early followers, were encouraged to seek God in places of retreat where they found the opportunity to dwell in God's presence. It might be advisable for us to seek to develop similar practices in such a way that we might enable

---

5. He does this by suggesting a kind of mystical theology that is open to the Spirit. However, in his latest work, he provides a useful adapted Barthian dialectical critique of it. His concept of liquid ecclesiology is based on the idea that God is always *beyond* the church, but at the same time God is at work *in* it. Culture leads to continuous change, requiring flexibility and adaptability in the church in order to keep in step with potential movements of the Spirit in society. Ward, *Liquid Ecclesiology*.

6. Isa 40:1–5; Luke 3:2.

7. Luke 4:1–13.

8. Matt 4:11.

9. Mark 6:31.

10. Luke 5:16.

11. Luke 5:16.

contemporary believers and faith-seekers to come aside from their normal lives, from time to time, to seek to commune with God. Having said this, God is not limited to thin places. God is present by his Spirit in all places.[12]

The incarnation of Christ and his ongoing incarnational presence through his people and his Spirit may be found anywhere at any time. So I need to make it clear that we are not suggesting that we seek to take people out of their daily life contexts to find Christ with them. Rather I suggest there is value in seeking thin places for retreat so that people can, from time to time, take stock of their lives without the normal disturbances of life interrupting this important pursuit. It is not an issue of choosing either one or another, but it is a question of including both together. A more balanced spiritual life seems to require "both and" not "either or."

Scholarly Assessments

Jürgen Habermas has indicated that many of the peoples in contemporary Western society have lost faith in secularism.[13] They have themselves began to turn back to religion or other forms of spiritual exploration. He terms this turn in society post-secular. Post-secular people are once more recognizing the fundamental spiritual architecture of their human faculties. The atheist zoologist Alister Hardy recognized the fundamental spiritual hardwiring in human psychology.[14] He realized it to be a part of the very genetic architecture of human nature, making humans spiritual as part of their deepest instincts. The neuro-theologian Andrew Newberg recognizes that the human brain is fundamentally a believing organ.[15] He considers that all human perceptions are based on the belief that the compelling presences perceived through our senses are in actuality real. This in itself requires us to have

---

12. Ps 139:7–9.
13. Habermas, "Secularism's Crisis of Faith."
14. Hardy, *The Spiritual Nature of Man*.
15. Newberg, and Walden, *How God Changes Your Brain*.

faith in our senses and beyond them in our spiritual sixth sense (to coin a common phrase).[16] The majority of Westerners are in some sense aware of their spiritual natures, but they do not, as Drane has demonstrated,[17] go to Christian churches to get their questions addressed. I believe that creating the possibility for post-secular faith-seeking people to go on guided retreats to thin spaces may help them to explore their spiritual desires, as well as to understand them better in the light of the presence of Christ. As a result, they may too seek to engage in new intentional behaviors of prayer, Scripture reading, and contemplation in their questing after God. Jesus encourages us to seek and then to find because God is a self-revealing being.[18] Spiritual questing would seem fundamental to human nature.

Case Example

A Christian leader I met in continental Europe shared one way that these kinds of missional retreats are being experimented with to help seeking people explore their underused spiritual faculties. About ten years ago he began to offer retreats to not-yet-Christian middle-aged business professionals so that they might find time and space to assess their lives. He did this in locations that had the qualities of thinness. He offered weekends, or whole week-long retreats where seeking professionals could experience stillness, quietude, and rest. He found that these retreats became popular with highly paid professionals. These were individuals who had reached the peak of their careers and were now preparing for retirement, having made their fortunes. He tried to keep the cost low, but he found that these professionals insisted on paying €2,000–3,000. They said this was a legitimate expense for their ongoing personal development.

---

16. Foster, *Wired for God? The Biology of Spiritual Experience.*
17. Drane, *Do Christians Know How to Be Spiritual?*
18. Drane, *Do Christians Know How to Be Spiritual?*

They also directed peers to join these retreats. Some of these individuals were open-minded and willing to explore spiritual practices, as well as in some cases coming to embrace the Christian faith. Professionals like this are among what Keith terms the "new marginalized." Facilitating retreats in so-called thin spaces may be an important means of sharing spiritual capital with these kinds of highly paid professionals. Retreats can become part of a spiritual capital, as it is seen as a legitimate part of their personal development. Such activities may prove to act as a means of bridging capital where meaningful spiritual exploration is provided for the new marginalized.

Co-Creating and Co-Authoring New Sacred Storied Places

Places where new memories are constructed for those we engage with may also emerge as part of our shared connections with them. These may not be thin places as such, but rather environments where new kinds of story-laden sacred memories of encounters with God might be invested. There is a triadic process of God at work with people in the places where they live to be found in the Old and New Testament documents. God, people, and place form a kind of trinity. God has a people of his own creation.[19] God meets them in places.[20] They go on a journey to a final place of destiny that is located in a deep relationship with their Creator.[21] Hence this triadic paradigm positions God, people, and place together, with the God of self-revelation imparting new meanings to the life-stories of people in concrete locations. Human identity is based on narratives and self-scripts that derive from them. A "self-script" is a term already partly discussed. It is used by transactional analysts to describe the stories people construct about themselves

---

19. Inge, *A Christian Theology of Place*.
20. Moltmann, *God in Creation*.
21. Heb 12:18–24.

that help them to make sense of their lives.[22] As a clinical and pastoral counsellor, I find this kind of insight useful to include in this account of how people form their identities with reference to the Christian story. People make sense of their lives in the light of the stories they tell themselves about who they are, where they come from, and where they think they are going. A "storied place" is a location that acts as a place of shared memories that draw people together to become part of the Christian story. It also means they will develop stories together leading to them forming shared identities, based on similar shared stories that in turn will help them to make sense of their faith-stories.

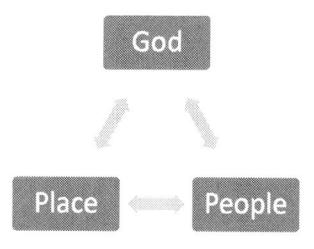

```
              God
             /   \
            /     \
         Place ⟷ People
```

These "storied places" (whatever shape or form they may take) may act as a means to join the stories of how people met God in a place of importance to the larger biblical narrative. The grand biblical metanarrative may be defined in terms of **c**reation, **f**all, **r**edemption, and **c**onsummation (CFRC). People may make sense of themselves as created by God for a purpose. The fall into sin makes sense of the present world, as it is mixed with good and evil. Redemption places those who accept Jesus Christ to become part of God's in-breaking kingdom. Consummation provides the goal of the Triune mission, where all peoples may become part of his soon-to-arrive eternal kingdom. As I have argued, a storied place helps people to link their stories to divine encounters with the still-speaking God.

It is not as such for us to create these places from nothing. A sacred storied place will probably come to consciousness as a

22. Pitman, *Transactional Analysis for Social Workers and Counsellors.*

location where God brought and brings meaning to people. It may be a meeting place like a coffee shop (a third place). The narratives invested in storied places will come about as people tell their stories in them related to how they first encountered God in them. Storied places are invested with meaning because God has chosen to reveal himself to people in them.

Creation → Fall → Redemption → Consummation

A storied place becomes a location invested with memories of what God has done there or revealed of himself there. For example, Soul Survivor UK moved one of its locations for its large festivals. Some of the youth leaders I spoke to in the new location did not feel the same sense of God's presence in the new location. This was almost certainly due to the lack of memories related to the old location that they carried in their psyches making the new location feel like it was bereft of them. We may invest in these places, seeking to memorialize God's work there. How can we help those we share life with to also develop storied places of special divine encounter in their communities?

Case Examples

New storied places need to be creatively invested with pictures, texts, and other artistic expressions of what a place means to the people who gather there. They can be located in the midst of neighborhoods, rather than separated from them. Obviously some people visit church buildings to find a sense of peace outside of the context of worship services that occur in them. So a sense of refuge from the frenetic strains of life may be what some experience in churches that have sacred art and architectural design features. We must not lose sight of this important contribution that sacred places like churches provide for some. However, many do not go to church buildings to benefit from its symbolic atmosphere, and they will probably respond much better to places located in their communities that symbolize what they sense to be sacred. This would seem to require that Christians might help them to develop new sacred memories suited to their context. God's people need to become salt and light in their everyday lives beyond their sacred buildings. God's people might help faith-seeking people to imagine how to represent their developing sense of awe of the divine in the places where they interact with missionary believers and start to realize the reality of the spiritual presence of Jesus for themselves.

In a missional café I know, a kind of new storied place is taking shape. Patrons of this café are coming to know it as a place of encounter with God's generosity. It is a place where people can confidentially share their challenges and receive discreet prayer, care, and support, as well as buying high quality food and drinks at low prices. Memories are being represented there by the crayon drawings of children placed on the café's walls. It is a comfortable and intimate friendly atmosphere of welcome and retreat. And, yes, people are coming to know something of God and his presence there. They keep on returning to be enriched by its positive atmosphere.

I have also engaged in research at an allotment church project. In this allotment local people can discover the God of creation and nature in their connection with the cultivation and growth of produce. There is more than one missional allotment I have visited. These projects too seem to be becoming storied places of a type where people encounter God in nature.

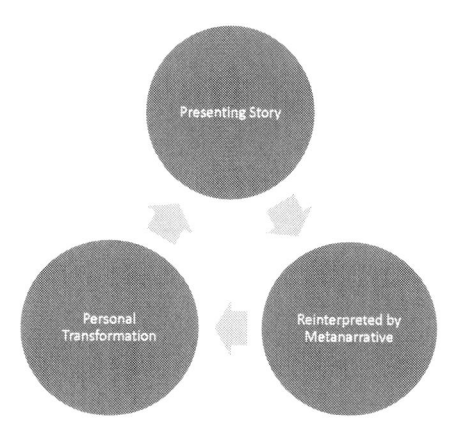

The majority of late-modern post-secular people do not go to sacred church buildings, but they do go to cafes, allotments, hotels, and conference centers, where they might experience a sense of escape, and at times retreat from their normal struggles and life challenges. We may need to reconceive how we might provide storied places and opportunities to experience thin places for the new marginalized.

Hearing God's Voice and Connecting with His Presence

How can we help post-secular people hear God's voice and find connection with God's presence? Are there practices and ways that we can facilitate for them to meet God in thin places or new missional storied places?

It seems obvious enough that we cannot make God speak to us. God cannot be programmed or activated by any human effort to communicate with us. However, biblical evidence demonstrates God's readiness and openness to communicate and commune with humans.[23] We cannot tell God what to say to us either. There is ancient and contemporary testimony of people who make time and space in their schedules to welcome communion with God.[24] We often term these practices as listening postures or rhythms of life that prepare us for communion and receptivity of heart and mind so we might converse with God. Jesus declared that God is more willing to give us his Holy Spirit than we are to ask for the divine presence.[25]

Even if the new marginalized do not realize it, often they seem to be seeking for some sort of resolution to tensions that exist between their lives of production and consumption, and the deeper call from within to discover the meaning to their lives. There seems to be a rift between the surface-level accumulation of

---

23. Bockmuehl, *Listening to the God Who Speaks*.
24. Deere, *Surprised by the Voice of God*.
25. Luke 11:13.

products and consumption of goods and the much deeper desires of the soul. A void needs filling with the God of Shalom.[26]

One way that we might help people to explore who they are and what life means might be through attentive active listening. We may need to develop the capacities to listen out for what God's Spirit might be inspiring within people.[27] This will take time, rapport building, and the development of friendships. I often use a four-phase model to track spiritual transformation in my life and that of others.

In phase one (see below), people might explore their current life-stories. In phase two, they might come to new understandings and reinterpretations of their stories in the light of the biblical and Christian story. In phase three, this might lead to new behaviors, actions, beliefs, and life-practices. We can act as facilitators who share in their life-journeys and help them to keep on exploring, understanding, and acting in new ways. This is a fundamental approach required for any helpful kind of spiritual exploration. The goal of active listening like this is to empower rather than manipulate people to explore what God might be calling them to do. Transformation will occur if people feel they have freedom to explore life with God without undue pressure being put on them to make hasty commitments. The fourth phase in this explorative journey will be to equip seekers to themselves become facilitators of spiritual transformation for others.

---

26. See on Groothuis, *Christian Apologetics*, 15–22.
27. Hardy, *Pictures of God*, 211–32.

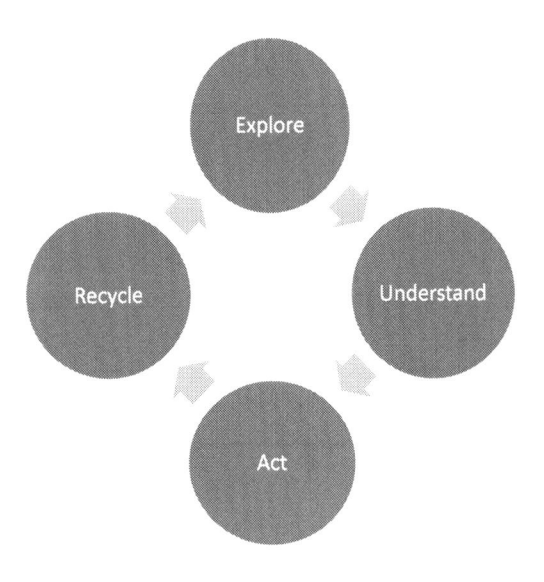

[Diagram: Four circles in a cycle — Explore → Understand → Act → Recycle → Explore]

I have at times related this four-phase model to what I have termed a four-phase resurrection model of spiritual transformation. I base it on the Pauline practical theology of baptism found in Romans chapter 6, and Egan's three-stage counselling model.[28] Paul writes:

> What shall we say then? Are we to continue in sin that grace may abound? By no means! How can we who died to sin still live in it? Do you not know that all of us who have been baptized into Christ Jesus were baptized into his death? We were buried therefore with him by baptism into death, so that as Christ was raised from the dead by the glory of the Father, we too might walk in newness of life.[29]

In phase one, we might take our start with Paul, who spoke of the life of a person before they entered into the watery symbolic baptismal grave, where they might share in Christ's death for their sins. It would bring them to the verge of forgiveness and acceptance in Christ. In phase one, at the edge of the watery grave of

28. Egan, *The Skilled Helper*.
29. Rom 6:1–4. RSV.

baptism, the seeker explores and assesses their present life-story. A key question will often be: what needs to be transformed in my life? Another may be: what do I need to leave behind at the water's edge? Symbolically each of us stand on the "verge of change." Faith-seekers will need to be helped to explore the Christian story and what it means for their future life-journey. This is the first phase in the process of transformation. The Spirit of Christ may be said to prepare seekers for the new Christian life and how the Christian story might inform their future life of following the Lord.

The second phase in the process, following Paul's baptism symbolism, is that people enter into and are buried under the watery grave. They intentionally repent of their old ways of life without Christ. They identify themselves with Christ leaving their old lives behind. New life from then on will be redefined by serving and following the Lord Jesus. This is a "deconstructive" phase, which is based on the real presence of God the Spirit to end the power of evil and sin as a dominant force in a new believer's life. It is here that new followers may discover the real power of Christ to end the hold of sin and evil. Of course, a lifelong journey continues afterwards where challenges to faith and the Christian life occur. However, allegiance to the God of the cross, in Pauline terms, is to intentionally put the old life behind us. It involves deep conversion, where the behaviors, habits, and old dysfunctional ways of living, thinking, and behaving are renounced. Old worldviews that did not have Christ in the center of them are deconstructed. A new identity is constructed in the light of the story and person of Christ.

The third phase in the process of transformation is that we are resurrected from the watery grave. It involves the emergence of a new consciousness of ourselves as now an eternal part of the kingdom of God. Future life will entail trust and obedience in following the king (of the kingdom). It is will be a journey that involves a continued ongoing process of dying and rising with Christ. Just as the journey begins with death and resurrection so it also commences as a spiritual practice of ongoing submission to the Lord. There is the need to continually seek to access the power of the new life found in communion with the indwelling Spirit of Jesus.[30] This phase involves "reconstructive transformation." Part of this includes a consciousness of our eternal security. Each believer needs to view themselves as those who belong to the family of God.[31] It means each of us no longer fear punishment or judgment at the hands of our Creator.[32]

A fourth phase, known as recycling, may be therefore posited. Each of us will keep on going through a process of lifelong transformation as we keep on following the living Christ of the Spirit. This process relates to the four-phase transformation model suggested below. Each of us will need to keep on going through iterations of this kind of transformational process over our lifetimes.

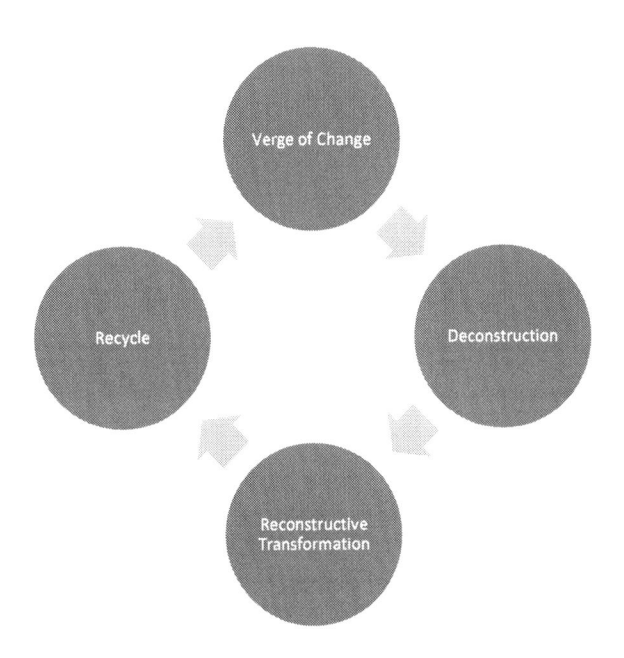

```
                    Verge of Change

        Recycle                       Deconstruction

                    Reconstructive
                    Transformation
```

---

30. Ross and Bevans, *Mission on the Road to Emmaus*, 24, 33, 43, 91, 101, 104, 154, 223, 229, 233, 236.

31. John 5:24.

32. 1 John 4:17.

Four-Phase Transformation Model	Four-Phase Resurrection Model
Explore: an exploration of the persons presenting life story seeking for evidence of the Spirit's work in it	*The verge of change:* the persons old existing life is assessed in the light of the Christian story. (Before entering waters of baptism and communion with God)
Understand: the seeker comes to a consciousness of themselves as in need of Christ and they are helped to reshape and reinterpret their life in the light of the biblical Christian story	*Deconstruction:* the person chooses to bury the old sinful ways of life and their former lives in the watery grave. They go through a process of deconstruction of what needs to change through a process of repentance and reinterpretation of their life stories in the light the gospel story. (Immersed under the watery grave)
Act: the seeker lives a new life as a conscious follower of Jesus behaving in new ways based on this new consciousness and an awareness of the Spirit's presence within them as their Lord, friend, and guide	*Reconstructive Transformation:* upon symbolically rising from the watery grave the person now begins to see themselves as an eternal part of the kingdom of God and as eternally belonging to God's family. Their fundamental identity is now to consider they belong inseparably to God's family. (Rises out of the watery grave)
Recycle: The new believer is equipped to make other disciples using the same practical approach to join with the work of the Spirit in other's lives	*Recycle:* The believer is equipped to help others become transformed in cooperation with the Spirit of Christ to go through this process—they will in one sense also go through this process for themselves again, repeatedly, at different levels as they grow and mature as they give every part of their lives over to Christ; as part of the work of the Spirit [known as sanctification] (Re-cycling involves the journey of faith and ongoing transformation throughout a lifetime's journey for each of us. None of us arrive in this life. The call to self-transcendence and going beyond our own limits, and finding new capacities to serve Christ, involves a lifelong as well as eternal journey of following him—in one sense, we never arrive because the infinite God is always beyond us beckoning us to follow)

| Four-Phase Transformation Model | Four-Phase Resurrection Model |

Rationale: Both of these models link together based on what I have termed a "listening-out process," where a believer "listens out" for evidence of the Spirit's work in a seeker's life (as they do in their own lives), and then helps them to develop a new consciousness of themselves as committed followers of Christ. Those who disciple new believers also need to equip them to become disciple-makers who can help others to reinterpret their life-stories in the light of the Jesus' story, based on the power of his presence in their souls. The goal will be to help them to use these same four-phase approaches reflexively (see below for a definition of this term). The strength of a basic process map, like this one, to help people in their journeys to become followers of Christ, is that it helps to chart how the Spirit may be said to transform spiritually seeking peoples. Every believer is called to missional ministry. This model is simple and can be learnt by those who have themselves been intentionally shaped and formed in this way.

Neither of these four-phase process models are programs to be used in mission. Rather, they need to be viewed as loosely held structural approaches to help us map spiritual transformation processes. Some of us may be ahead of others in our life-long journey of following Jesus. What we have is more experience of taking the journey, which we can pass on.

However, this puts more mature followers in a place of responsibility that should be taken on with a great deal of humility. We might use either of these models to help us chart our own journeys as the Spirit transforms our life-stories. We may be said to need to engage in reflexive spiritual practices using reflective models something like these. (The pastoral cycle is yet another model.) Reflexivity requires that we not only reflect on the impact of others on us, but also for us to reflect on our impact on others. Are we faithfully following the Lord Jesus in an ongoing journey of self-transcendence? Are we going beyond our old sinful natures to become increasingly like Christ? Our call may be considered to include the discernment of the Spirit's work in us, as well as to entail our participation in the mission of God. Reflexivity requires that we consider the impact of the Spirit on our lives and on that of others. We might often ask ourselves how we could better interact with others as we seek to follow what Christ is calling us to do alongside them.

We will inevitably need to underpin intentional disciple-making ministry with a deep commitment to work with people at the point of greatest need as this is where the incarnational Spirit of Christ will begin to shape and form them. It will be this very process of working in the immediate context that is the basis to all our journeying with others. As we journey with others we will also have the privilege of helping them to develop their own self-scripts and their own interpretations of how their stories are part of the Christian story.

As a pastoral counselor I have often observed some believers seem to miss the proverbial log in their own eye. Instead, all of us at some time in our journeys are all too willing to focus on the speck in another's eye.[33] We might provide an example from a psychological perspective. Each of us develop our identities partly by saying what we are not. To do this we give examples from other's lives of what we are *not*. We say, in other words, "we are not like this group because we do not do things their way." This is known as "othering." We are not like "those others," in other words.[34] We represent ourselves by saying what we are *not*. There is a dangerous spiritual pathology that can arise from this tendency if it becomes our primary way of identifying ourselves. We may set ourselves up to define who we are by judging other's stories and outlooks as in some sense a threat to our own identity. Some people seem to be constantly on the lookout in others for what they consider to be wrong about their views, beliefs, and values, etc. In other words, we may define ourselves based on a resistance identity.[35]

Unfortunately, if we define our identities by what we are not, then we may exist not to follow Christ but to protect ourselves. It is really a subtle control mechanism that keeps us safe from the work of the Spirit of Christ who calls us to go beyond our need to control our own lives. If we lose the things we live to resist then we may lose a reason for our faith. Surely a more grounded healthy spirituality might entail learning how to let go and to rise up above our present

---

33. Matt 7:3–5.
34. Holliday, Hyde, and Kullman, *Intercultural Communication*, 23–38.
35. Castells, *The Power of Identity*.

horizons. We might speak of flying in the Spirit. By this analogy I would suggest we need to seek to be empowered by the inner life of the Spirit of Christ to have courage not to just be satisfied with the status quo.[36] Thin places can provide those times when one bigger than our own horizons can reveal new depths and new journeys for us to take. We may start to view other parts of the divine meta-horizon with the eyes of the prophet. God is surely much bigger than our limited horizons. How high are you hovering above the ground? How free are you in your faith journey? How much control do you require of yourself and others around you?

Creating Hospitable Places Where There Is Freedom to Explore and Grow

We will consider two accounts of the themes of the generosity and hospitality of God from Luke and Acts. In the Gospel we find the oft-cited narrative of the prodigal sons (Luke 15:11–32). The youngest son does what was unheard of in the patriarchal structures of most ancient Near Eastern families. He asked for his inheritance from his father before his father's passing. The father in this story already exhibits an almost ridiculous level of grace and generosity to this son when he gives him his inheritance. The son then leaves home and dishonors his family name by spending his inheritance on prostitutes, food, drink, and a lack of ethically based living. He later returns home. His father has evidently been looking out in hope for him to return each day. He recognizes his son in the distance. The son's declaration to his father demonstrates his realization that he is no longer deserving of being treated like a son. The father's generosity and hospitality knows no bounds it seems. He welcomes his son home. He generously welcomes him fully back into his family. No conditions or strings are attached. It is opulent generous grace. The father's hospitality and generosity are based on the joy that this son who was dead to the family is

---

36. Karkkainen, *Pneumatology*, 96.

now alive again,[37] he was lost to his family but now has been found. The older brother does not share in his father's gracious, generous, and hospitable spirit. He complains of ill treatment.[38] The main aspect of this parable to focus on is the outrageous grace, generosity, and hospitality of the father. He, like Father God, welcomes all of his people home. They are made part of God's ridiculously generous family. There is boundless grace and hospitality on offer.

This story is incredibly counter-cultural to the late-modern Western world where consumption and making a profit are the highest of ideals. For a missional community to be effective in third places a key question might be, in what ways might we model this ridiculous grace to others in acts of kindness and hospitality?

Luke, the theological editor of the Gospel, crafted these kinds of narratives providing insights into what Christ had to communicate about the prime values of God's kingdom. It has long been recognized that a focus in his accounts of the Lord's life and that of the early church in the book of Acts is on the universal soteriological aims of the mission of Jesus.[39] His accounts depict the grace, generosity, and hospitality of God towards all who will respond to his invitation to become part of God's family. This includes the outcasts of society,[40] those who are depressed, downcast, oppressed, possessed, weak, vulnerable, and poor,[41] as much as it includes the marginalized rich like Zacchaeus.[42] The ongoing mission of the Spirit of Jesus' (Acts 16:6–10) includes everyone in principle being given opportunities to become part of God's all-inclusive family. However, as Jesus noted, the harvest is great, but more workers are needed to bring in the harvest.[43] God's hospitality awaits each of us.

---

37. Byrne, *The Hospitality of God: A Reading of Luke's Gospel*. 85.

38. Luke 15:11–32.

39. Byrne, *The Hospitality of God*, 13, 15, 24–26, 45–46, 94, 100, 136, 147, 210.

40. Neyrey, *The Social World of Luke-Acts*, 135, 144, 164, 169, 227–28, 268–88, 378.

41. Neyrey, *The Social World of Luke-Acts*, 232.

42. Luke 19:1–10.

43. Matt 9:35–38.

Chapter 9

A Case in Question—Enhancing Community and Talking Jesus

KEITH FOSTER

Introduction

Bethel Church is an independent church that was set up in 1937 out of an evangelistic tent campaign that visited the city of Coventry, UK.[1] This was the last church to be planted in what was a prolific national evangelistic campaign that took place between 1928 and 1937. David Watts has written an insightful history of the "Bethel movement" that saw eighty-eight churches planted within this period, with some fifty-seven of those still active. The Coventry church sits on an artery of the city's ring road, a few minutes from the city center, adjacent to a local inner-city estate. Spon End is typical of many inner-city estates in the UK with many people defining the area as an undesirable place to live, often pointing to its measured levels of deprivation.[2] For

1. www.bethelchurch.org.uk.
2. Such sites as Datashine.org.uk give detailed statistics on areas of deprivation (education, health, disability, employment, etc.).

many years, the church largely relied on an attractional program of church-based ministries that were aimed to both meet the needs of local people and to attract them to its building. Recent years have seen a shift from such an approach to one that is based upon a missio Dei theology.[3] Such a theological shift has transitioned the church to one that sees itself in partnership with the God of mission within its local community as opposed to seeing its own program as the key missional driver. This has led to several ministry expressions aimed at the church becoming a presence within the local community.

One such initiative is the Oasis Café, which in the early years had been the initiative of the local Elim church. Over time, the vision of Elim for its use lessened as they sensed a new direction for them as a city church. Thus, in June 2016, following discussions with Bethel Church, a new vision was set for a community café that would sit in the heart of the local area to become a platform for community life and gospel living. The café was set up in order to provide a place for the local people in Spon End to come, where together with the café volunteers they could develop a sense of community and belonging. Additionally, Bethel Church, coming out of its evangelical tradition, was keen for the café to have an unashamed gospel distinctiveness, with not only cooks and servers volunteering at the café, but also café hosts whose passion and purpose was to share and show the love and message of Jesus to others. Over the summer of 2017, a pilot empirical research project was undertaken to assess the first-year impact of the café in two main areas:

(a) Its impact on the sense of community

(b) Its impact on the views of faith

Between June and October 2017, empirical pilot research was carried out in the form of individual structured questionnaires

---

3. Andrew Hardy is currently carrying out extensive research into this transition—see "How a Ministerial Education Programme with a Very Distinctive Ethos Has Helped Leaders to Begin to Develop a New Living Tradition in a Church."

and semi-structured interviews with regular users of the café. The questionnaire was divided into two main sections under "community well-being" and "attitude to faith." The "community well-being section" was devised to assess the developmental attitudes to the sense of community, both in general and specifically since their attendance at the café. The "attitude to faith" section was devised to assess general attitudes to the staff and more specifically faith conversations that may have taken place during their time of attending the café. Immediately following this was a ten- to fifteen-minute semi-structured interview that was aimed at drawing out thicker and more meaningful statements from the participants. The overall results from this early survey were encouraging with regards the impact of the café on the overall sense of community. All of the participants felt that their sense of community had been enhanced and saw the café as a place of community-value beyond the things they simply purchased and consumed.

With regards to faith conversations, while not all had experienced a direct conversation or challenge with regards to faith, all had an awareness of the faith and ethos of the volunteer team. Out of those whom had experienced direct faith conversations, the majority said they were open to hear about faith again with a number stating how they had felt a sense of challenge, considering themselves on a "journey" of discovery.

The semi-structured interviews revealed much more with regards to the impact of the café on the sense of community and attitudes toward faith. A selection of statements included:

> "The staff are really friendly, this is a great place."

> "This is our café, it fits in with our context, especially as it is opposite the school."

> "A good little café—a safe place to chat about things."

> "It's good this is a local space—if this was in a church or something, then people might not go as they might be set in their ways."

> "This café is full of admirable people. Why would you want to be with people who drag you down? You don't look down on people unless you are picking them up."
>
> "It's a good idea for faith groups to create public spaces where the faith community is accessible."
>
> "Seeing the way people [the Christians] interact with each other in the café and with other customers—it is not an 'ordinary' café—it encourages that confidence to seek help and to 'look deeper' into faith."

The creation of this "place" with the dual aim of enhancing the sense of local community while maintaining a gospel intentionality makes this an interesting place where theories of place, belonging, progressive localism, and faith can be assessed. Further studies are taking place across a broader range of café projects and various communities that will seek to reveal how such objectives might co-exist, asking such questions as: What tensions can this create? What negotiated "trade-offs" might take place between maintaining and enhancing community yet doing so with a conversionist agenda?

Interestingly, the potential for local places (outside of welfare provision) to provide spaces for developing an enhanced sense of belonging and community are not the initiative of the church alone. In September 2017, the BBC news website reported on the increasing "café culture"[4] where such places provide a regular place of community interaction for many who otherwise might be isolated. The interesting thing about the Oasis Café coming out of its evangelical tradition, driven by a gospel intentionality, is that the regular clients do not see faith-motivation as a barrier, indeed early comments suggest that this (for a number of regulars at least) has tapped into a much richer, broader sense of secular spiritual capital and faith exploration.

Of course, the alternative might be for the church to insist on trying to persuade people within our communities to enter our unfamiliar places (places unfamiliar to them that is). The question

---

4. http://www.bbc.co.uk/news/in-pictures-41244294.

is that while we (as Christ-followers) might feel more comfortable ourselves within our church buildings, are we willing to become "uncomfortable" and enter or develop a local community place that might create a more familiar platform for our communities? Uncomfortable places do not lend themselves to easy conversations.

Practical Community Projects through an Evangelical Lens

In order to assess one's approach and where one wants to go, it is essential to know "where we are" now. People rarely think about the lens and underlying culture through which they see and approach life. Whilst the evangelical core tenets of biblicism, crucicentrism, activism, and conversionism are important, it might be helpful to also see any potential barriers and constraints that our beliefs and faith-culture might create.

Evangelicalism as a tradition is very broad, with many groups (Reformed Baptists, Pentecostals, Independent, et al.) claiming to sit under this banner. Among the four tenets of Bebbington's "special marks," biblicism often plays the leading role, informing the approach to the other three. The overriding authority of Scripture over everything, including the church, lays at the heart of the sola scriptura debate during the reformation.[5] This centrality of Scripture legacy is a strong hallmark of many evangelical churches, and while Bethel Church Coventry, for example, is developing a new missiological approach to the local community, based on a missio Dei understanding,[6] this biblicist emphasis still underpins its self-understanding. Understanding a church's hermeneutic and the forming "stories" that impact their horizons and practices is essential. Orthodoxy impacts orthopraxy.

My own story of conversion was from an "unchurched" background into a charismatic Elim tradition. Following several years within the military, which interrupted exposure to church of any

---

5. George, *Theology of the Reformers*.
6. Flett, *The Witness of God*, 35–77.

particular "flavor," I subsequently spent twenty-four years within a Reformed evangelical church gaining an understanding and appreciation of the "special" evangelical marks. These served to underpin my earlier charismatic experiences while also giving me an appreciation of a biblicist hermeneutic. While overall I found this to be positive and enriching, I also became acutely aware of the dangers of a misplaced biblicist emphasis on cultural separatism with regards the "church" and the "world." A biblical mandate for a church to possess a good contextual theological and missiological approach to its community was needed. Yet sadly for many, the protection of the purity of the Bible (the "Word") and their ongoing tradition can be the greater emphasis. While many evangelical churches may (considering the picture of Peter in Acts chapter 10)[7] still be in a "trance" while endeavoring to work out the vision they have been given (in all its unappealing traditional counter-culturalism), encouragingly Bethel Church has made some significant inroads in its approach to the local community and beyond with both a missional and practical theological approach.

Practical theology does what it says on the tin, it seeks to be practical, analyzing the relationship between orthodoxy (right teaching) and orthopraxy (right practice). However, the criticism often levelled at practical theology is that in its practical emphasis, it gives scarce attention to the Bible. A 2011 meeting of the British and Irish Association of Practical Theologians (BIAPT) came to a general agreement that "the relationship between the Bible and practical theology (was) an uneasy one."[8] Within this group a wide and rich variety of methods of engaging with Scripture within a practical theological and theological reflective framework were presented and discussed, including lectio divina, contextual Bible study, scriptural reasoning, and theological reflection, amongst others. Following on from this, a 2012 symposium to discuss this very issue of the Bible and practical theology took place, where

---

7. In Acts chapter 10, while in a trance, Peter is given the vision of the sheet three times.

8. Bennett and Rogers, *Report on Bible and Practical Theology Symposium*.

each delegate was asked to bring and present a biographical paper to the discussion. In a rich and varied meeting that addressed the challenges of Bible inclusion within practical theology, Ladd saw the need to challenge the evangelical position of a simple applied theological approach to the Bible and stated his desire "to see evangelicals moving away from the traditional applied theology model... to allow for a more nuanced approach to the authority of Scripture."[9] In a 2013 paper on the use of Scripture within practical theology, Mark Cartledge came to the worrying conclusion that "the majority of the authors in academic practical theology either use Scripture in a limited manner or not at all."[10] Cartledge identifies this as an issue and gap between those parts of the academy that use Scripture sparingly and the many Christians for whom the Bible

> ... permeates their existence through daily prayer and weekly worship (and where they) cannot escape this theologically defined worldview in which biblical texts, ideas, and stories are embedded.[11]

Such tensions have often led to the withdrawal of the evangelical community from discussions occurring in the theological academy. It is easier when the place we are serving is a familiar and comfortable one. Perhaps the concern and potential of being "labelled" as liberal, or even heretical, by engaging with such disciplines has prevented many evangelicals from entering the conversation.

Practical theology sees theological reflection and the social sciences join together. The insights from social science can provide valuable and practical approaches and methodologies for the researcher, however the perceived barrier for those viewing the world through a biblicist lens is to be found where "often the account given about a given subject is more informed by social

---

9. Bennett and Rogers, *Report on Bible and Practical Theology Symposium*.

10. Cartledge, "The Use of Scripture in Practical Theology."

11. Cartledge, "The Use of Scripture in Practical Theology," 280.

science than by theology."[12] Theology, and more specifically biblical insights, can be few and far between, with many contextual biblical considerations being built upon a weak platform of selective and convenient proof-texts.

This said, in as much as it is important within an evangelical biblicist framework to demonstrate a sound regard and use of Scripture within such research, the evangelical academy itself also needs to be challenged to consider its function within practical theology if not indeed the wider secular academy. Stephen Pattison in his essay "Can We Speak of God in the Secular Academy? Or, Need Theology Be So Useless?"[13] addresses this question of bringing a theological voice to the secular academy, asking whether theology has, "any contribution to make."[14] Pattison identifies one of the issues of theology (or rather the issues of the secular academy with theology, as suspicions work both ways!) as its close association with institutional Christian religion, an association that "makes it deeply suspect."[15] While Pattison is commenting here from a perceived secular academic viewpoint, practical theologians aware of such suspicions might well (even subconsciously) adjust their approach to their research, even finding themselves tempted to significantly reduce how the Bible informs their projects, or at best offer some token biblical texts of semi-relevance, in order to make their research more palatable or credible to secular colleagues or peers. Pattison challenges theologians to come out from under their institutional umbrellas, with their sole focus on their own traditions and authoritative texts, to additionally engage with and study "matters of contemporary and human concern."[16]

As I reflect on the challenge, I am reminded of a passage found within Scripture, found within the 10th and 11th chapters of the New Testament book of Acts. Peter is given a vision that will both challenge his scriptural worldview, informed by Torah, and

12. Cartledge, "The Use of Scripture in Practical Theology," 280.
13. In Pattison, *The Challenge of Practical Theology*, 197–211.
14. Pattison, *The Challenge of Practical Theology*, 197.
15. Pattison, *The Challenge of Practical Theology*, 198.
16. Pattison, *The Challenge of Practical Theology*, 199.

subsequently call him to engage with a new community (the gentile community represented by Cornelius). Following both his experience and research,[17] Peter is then called to present his findings to the wider church.[18] Perhaps as the evangelical church strives to endeavor to understand the social capital of its local community, with a view to contextualizing the gospel within that community, using practical theological and reflective methods to do so may be helpful. As Peter presented his findings and the Acts church reflected together, the encouraging research outcome, instead of entrenching their separatist position, led to the church concluding, "So then, even to gentiles, God has granted repentance that leads to life."[19]

Enhancing Community with a Gospel Intentionality

Having said all that, it is necessary to emphasize the necessity of not only desiring to improve and enhance our communities but doing so *while maintaining the gospel vision*, for Scripture tells us that "without a vision, the people perish." Chester's previously quoted caution is worth repeating. Acts of kindness and community service without gospel declaration lead to the danger of becoming, "sign posts pointing nowhere." Jesus, speaking to the Samaritan woman, recorded in the 4th chapter of John, gives us a perfect example. Jesus' mission into Samaria was already breaking all of the "rules"; to then speak to a Samaritan woman would simply add insult to injury. While Jesus was comfortable with the situation, his disciples (verse 27) and even the woman (verse 9) felt the social tension. While practicalities of "food and drink" provided the context for the discussion, the real point of meaning for this community was to see Jesus as the "bread and water" of life. Such was the impact of Jesus on the woman that she went

17. Acts 10:9–48.
18. Acts 11:1–18.
19. Acts 11:18.

back to her town to encourage others to "come and see" (verse 29). Incarnating within the local community allows such conversations to take place. It is very unlikely that conversations within our local community will take place with everyone, but news travels fast. As the Holy Spirit of mission brings people into the community-places where God's people are, our Christ-centered conversations with individuals can have a much broader impact within our communities as people are encouraged to "come and see."

Chapter 10

How Phoenix Church Equips Urban Missionaries

Andrew Hardy

Introduction

This chapter will focus on a case study of a church called Phoenix, which has moved from being a traditional dynastic church to becoming a church that intentionally seeks to create a consciousness of the mission of God among its people. The key question I address in this chapter relates how Phoenix Church has been shaped to equip members to become urban-facing missionaries in some notable cases, despite the churches earlier dynastic inward-looking structures. A dynastic church is defined as one that is controlled by one or two strong families who form a kind of ruling dynasty. According to Croft, dynastic church structures have some families that tend to be in the primary positions of leadership and decision making.[1] For the most part, members who belong to these congregations will tend to conform to the decisions that the dynasty makes for them. The exercise of authority

---

1. Croft, *Transforming Communities*, 50.

and the imposition of decisions on the congregation is employed by the dynasty either through positional power, coercive power, or persuasive power. I have discussed the dynamics of the exercise of these kinds of power more fully elsewhere.[2] Simply stated, these three kinds of power may be defined as:

Positional power: The families who make up the dynasty most often have been in the church for many years. Their position is guaranteed by their history as protectors of the tradition. They are put in the position of power. Hence, by having this role-definition, they are empowered by the congregation to make decisions in the overall running of the church;

Coercive power: The families who are in the position of power might at times use coercion and manipulation to seek to control those who do not readily conform to their will. If people resist them, or seek not to conform, they are often marginalized and may end up leaving a congregation. Alternatively, they may choose to comply and no longer resist, or they may still attend but become bitter or discouraged;

Persuasive power: This often occurs when a dynasty has a member with charisma and persuasive abilities who is able to motivate members to do what is required by the dynasty.

A common profile of a dynastic church is that when a pastor is selected for ministry, she or he is expected to become a chaplain to the dynasty, to serve their needs, requirements, and demands. In these kinds of congregations a pastor is sought who will conform to the will of the dynasty. If she or he does not then a power struggle may ensue. It will often be the case that the minister will end up conforming to the dynasty's point of view. They may experience burn-out, or at times leave feeling discouraged and undermined. Alternatively dynasty members may protest and leave if they lose their power and influence. Another outcome may be a rift in the church. This kind of schism inevitably will lead to some

---

2. Hardy, Whitehouse, and Yarnell, *Power and the Powers*.

people leaving as they follow the dynasty or the pastor to join them elsewhere.

Moreover, a dynasty church has the expectation that the pastor is there to serve the congregation. It is her or his role to care for members. This position means she or he takes on responsibility to be what might be termed one of the "professional Christians," who are the specialized gospel preachers and evangelists. Leaders are often employed by non-missionally-engaged congregations to do mission *on their behalf*. As one church member put it, "After all, that's what we pay them for."

Conversely, members have the role to financially fund this kind of professional ministry. This will at some level be part of the conscious, or unconscious, attitudes and expectations of members in these kinds of faith communities. Phoenix Church was a dynastic church for many years, according to those who know it well. It was initially planted by a pioneer evangelist. But this pioneering start did not shape this church's later self-understanding. Rather than adopting a pioneering approach, where members might continue to help in planting yet other new churches, it became consolidated as a dynastic church. In this chapter, we will consider Phoenix Church's journey to the point where it has now been considerably transformed as a community that is seemingly enabling people to discover their missional calling.

New and Old Themes Merge and New Themes Emerge

There are four main reasons for choosing to code name the church discussed in this chapter as Phoenix. In the first instance, the church in early 2000 was burnt down. The church that arose from the ashes might be metaphorically related to the mythical bird, the Phoenix. The congregation's way of life has changed considerably since this fire. Secondly, Phoenix Church was planted in evangelistic work in the 1930s that arose out of the Welsh revival. After the evangelist from Wales departed, the new church that had been planted lost much of its fervor for evangelism. It was only after the fire that it began, like the Phoenix, to arise and to reconnect with its evangelistic roots. Thirdly, the 1930s campaign witnessed numerous churches planted throughout the UK, including a Bible training school, which was set up with the goal to equip leaders for ministry. Sadly this college failed within about eighteen months of starting.

In this case, unknown to the present pastor, he and his team were reconnecting with another of Phoenix Church's roots. They decided to establish a leaders' and members' training school in the church in order to equip them for local mission. It has now been running for about six years. It, unlike the earlier college, has successfully trained leaders and members who are continuing to serve their local communities or other churches with their mission efforts. Once more, the mystical Phoenix bird of the Spirit has arisen from the ashes to new life. Spiritual revivification for this church has meant that some of its people are practically seeking to engage in mission and ministry in their urban contexts. A key goal in Phoenix is to enable everyone who is willing to become disciple-makers. It requires that they first are equipped as disciples to discern and participate in the ongoing mission of the Spirit of Jesus.

In this chapter, we will trace some of the important themes that my research has revealed about how this church has been transformed, from being a dynastic church, where the members were not empowered or equipped for participation in local mission, to becoming a church where some members are increasingly coming to a consciousness of themselves as those called to participate in the mission of God.

In this fourth sense, the Phoenix arises from the ashes in similitude to revivalism that occurred in the city it is found in. Revival fires were part of its early Pentecostal heritage. A kind of revival is occurring again, grounded in the equipping of members for missional ministry through this church's training academy. The difference between what is occurring among them now, compared to when Phoenix Church was first planted, is that every member is being encouraged to seek to participate in the mission of God. It is not reliant on one charismatic evangelist's gifts.

It has often been the church-planting charismatic leader and evangelist that has been part of an evangelical ideal. The services of the professional evangelizer can discourage the people they lead by creating an impression that experts are the proper people to do the work of gospel mission. Charismatically gifted leaders who possess strong personalities, including impressive communication abilities, may seem impossibly gifted. By comparison, we may come to view ourselves ill-equipped to share our faith with others. Even more troubling has been the historical tendency to put these gifted individuals on a pedestal, which can tend to discourage people from engaging in personal evangelism because of their perceived inferiority. This kind of thing has potentially hindered God's people from becoming active participants in God's evangelical mission.

The result has often been that once such an evangelist leaves a new church plant its members have not been equipped to be missional in their own right. In the missional church formation occurring in Phoenix, what puts the feet on its local missionary efforts is that members are intentionally being encouraged to make disciples of others. In other words, they are coming to conceive of themselves as part of the mobile missional body of Christ. The pastor of Phoenix Church has intentionally discouraged members from putting him in the place of the expert Christian. Instead, he has emphasized that he is called to equip them to become the hands and feet of Jesus. This type of leadership seeks to increase the work of Christ among God's people. Conversely a goal is to decrease the focus on the church leader as the preferred expert in ministry. This is an important finding in my research with Phoenix.

This is why I believe the largest missional challenge facing the church is to enable *all* of God's people to have a consciousness of themselves as followers of the living Jesus sent out to make disciples of others. If missional leaders and their missional teams do not intentionally do this, I believe we will have churches that are missional in name but they will essentially rely on paid leaders to be the primary missionaries. A critique I make of the missional church conversation is that it is still essentially seeking to operate without empowering ordinary members (each of us) to become conscious of themselves as missionaries.

Themes in the Shaping of Phoenix Church

It is important to recognize that it is the Spirit of Christ at work through missional leaders that might lead to the effective equipping of God's people. I know from bitter experience what happens if a team seeks to impose its will on a church. Forced kinds of so-called missional change management can actually *undermine* change in churches. Desire for change needs to arise from the congregation perceiving that this is what God is calling them to engage in undertaking. Fundamental to all transformation of faith-communities is the need for the people in them to discern, sense, and to pursue the Spirit's call to follow Christ in his ongoing mission. This requires the development of spiritual discernment in the life-practices of every follower of Christ. A passion to do this very thing has been part of the fieldwork accounts my investigation has revealed among some Phoenix Church members.

A good missional leadership team must surely "actively listen out" for responses from believers for what the Spirit is inspiring within them. Roxburgh and Romanuk suggest this to be the most effective approach to use to help a church undertake missional transformation.[3] The goal is not to implant a new missional DNA as such, this would be manipulation. A better strategy might be to encourage people to gather around the Scriptures in order to listen out for how the Spirit might inspire their missional imaginations. It is suggested that if congregants do not discern this call for themselves, then any seeming transformation will only run surface deep. I fear that poor missional change management processes implemented in some churches means that the missional church movement might only be one inch thick and twenty miles wide in

---

3. Roxburgh and Romanuk, *The Missional Leader*.

terms of its real missional impact among ordinary church members. People need to be inspired to go much deeper. Inspiration will then hopefully flow out from deep within, thus motivating congregants to participate in what Christ is doing among their friends and colleagues. This will thicken the depth of missional impact, but it will also narrow down the expansiveness of many of a missional church's efforts. Jesus seemingly spoke of this deeper type of spiritual engagement as rivers of water flowing out of the bellies of his followers.[4]

The Spirit might be best claimed to work in our missional efforts if we engage in *deep* friendships with *fewer* faith-seeking people but with *much more intentional* pouring into their lives. I fear that much of the missional church conversation rhetoric is not founded on properly grounded research into deeper missional relationships that really change people for the longer-term journey of following Christ. Joining with the Spirit's lifeblood in amongst those we work among will then hopefully vivify and empower ordinary members to participate in all that God inspires within them.

In our work with the US-founded Bonhoeffer Discipleship Project,[5] Keith and I have recognized that a believer's call and conversion has historically been separated from discipleship, especially in the evangelical tradition. Like Bonhoeffer, we recognize that authentic disciples pay a high price when they completely give their allegiance to Jesus. Disciples need to count the cost of following Christ.[6] Contemporary consumer culture often focuses the work of churches on meeting consumer needs rather than developing sacrificial living and whole-life costly allegiance to Jesus, the Lord. Conversion that leads to believers calling themselves "saved" might develop into an identity that can be expressed as: "I am called to work and live out my life in the knowledge of my

---

4. John 7:38–39.
5. The Bonhoeffer Discipleship Project was founded by Bill Hull and Brandon Cook.
6. Bonhoeffer, *The Cost of Discipleship*.

saved status. It is the role of the paid and trained clergy to care for the needs of me and my family."

We might also identify the required response from the employed minister, requiring of them that they identify themselves to act as service providers. Members and leaders together may exist in this matrices of identity, as the ones who earn money to pay the minister to engage in professional ministry and mission on their behalf. Phoenix Church was very much like this prior to its more recent journey towards becoming a missionary-equipping congregation.

It is interesting that some members at Phoenix Church still hold the older view of the assigned roles of members and ministers. It was formerly a very large part of its identity, especially prior to the church fire of early 2000. Several of those interviewed expressed the view that their role was to earn money to pay for the services of the minister. A few commented that it is not every member's role to be engaged in mission, or for them or others to make disciples. I respect their honesty and integrity for averring this view. We need to take these views seriously. These too are often the views of the majority of church-goers, even if they do not consciously express them. But in actual fact, in practice, most church-goers do not engage in what the early followers of Jesus naturally did, which is really Keith's and my main point. These early followers seemed to intentionally seek to make disciples of others.[7] Have things changed that much, making the seemingly normative accounts of the New Testament for the Christian life no longer authoritative?[8]

Despite some Phoenix members still not seeing themselves as those called and sent by a missionary God, there is a new theme

---

7. The Gospel of Matthew was probably written with a specific Jewish Christian community in mind. Matthew may have sought to position this community's primary mission to be that of making disciples of non-Jews, not only Jews (Matt 28:16–20). However, I assume this kind of missionary disciple-making focus for a community like this. Clearly this is a view, not a fact we can confirm.

8 For a case that the NT does expect all Christians to engage in mission, please see the appendix.

that has emerged in the congregation since the church fire. Quite a number of those interviewed talked with clear passion and determination about their feelings of the challenge to engage in what they perceived God to be calling them to do. It would be a pipe dream in any church undergoing missional transformation to expect everyone to see things the same way. A clear majority of about 70 percent of the church seem to be at different stages on the journey to becoming more engaged in seeking to participate in mission in their everyday life contexts. There are four identifiable groups who are in what might be termed a spectrum of an emerging new missional identity. We might trace these four points of reference in a spectrum or bandwidth (to use the language of physics). They are:

Band One: Those Counting the Cost

The people of God need more than can be provided in Sunday worship services to become authentic followers of Christ. It requires that they are apprenticed to a more experienced follower of Christ to be mentored, shaped, and formed to themselves become effective disciple-makers. If nothing else, a Sunday service needs to be about more than corporate worship. It also needs to be the arena in which people are challenged to count the cost of following Jesus. Shaping them to become the kinds of disciples who can make disciple-makers of others needs to happen elsewhere beyond what is offered on Sunday mornings. Phoenix Church seeks to provide an environment of challenge to count the cost of following Christ in its worship services and preaching. However, the real transformation happens outside of the Sunday morning service context through Phoenix's training school. Moreover, the training school is in partnership with the Bonhoeffer Discipleship Project to shape leaders who can disciple others to themselves become missional disciple-makers. This means that people are engaged in mentoring and training with those who are already on the journey as disciple-makers themselves to become the same. This requires not a program but a process.

Hence, at Phoenix Church mission equipping begins with every Sunday morning being the place where the missional waters are stirred and people are challenged to count the cost. This happens as part of a fulsome biblically based diet of good robust teaching and preaching. Phoenix Church does not exist to make people feel comfortable. It exists to stir them up to become more than those who come to be cared for. It is also a place where they can be cared for and supported, but the larger goal is to empower every member to understand their own missional vocation, which will mean serving each other in love and deep, meaningful friendships. During fieldwork research interviews I listened to numerous accounts of those who were feeling challenged, who were also counting the cost of what it really means to be a follower of Christ. As I suggested, about 70 percent of the congregation realizes this challenge to one degree or another. The church is arguably at a critical tipping point to become a missional equipping agent that will be able to equip God's people for works of service.

Keith wrote in the last chapter that the goal of mission in third places is that we equip God's people with gospel intentionality. The goal of mission like this requires much more than simply to win converts who can become part of a holy huddle. A lifelong journey of following Christ, and making disciples of others, is also required. Phoenix Church exists in the urban context of a city. It seeks first of all to stir people up to re-interpret themselves as followers and disciple-makers sent to make disciples of others. They have spiritual capital invested deeply into their lives by this process, which others can then draw on as a kind of spiritual bank account. Hence, missional disciples are challenged to count the cost of following a much more challenging version of a missionary Jesus at Phoenix. This is very much a counter-cultural trend.

It challenges much of the evangelical middle-class ideology, where well-healed evangelicals make money and fund professional clergy to do what they need to really be doing themselves. This may sound harsh. However, it does seem to be part of a certain brand of evangelicalism. It is costly and counter-cultural to call for *all* of God's people to re-orientate their lives around themselves being completely given over to be ambassadors for Christ. And this needs to include God's people seeking to be missional in their preferred professions. Mission in the work place is very much part of mission in third places.

A considerable number of those interviewed in Phoenix have shared how people have been challenged to count the cost of being called to go out to where they sense Christ is sending them. This has been costly to Phoenix, as some people have left the congregation for a variety of reasons, often because they do not want to be part of a church that is calling them to service and mission. Having said this, some leavers have been interviewed who have been empowered, equipped, and encouraged to actually move their locations to go to work in mission in a ward of the city to which God has guided them. In these cases, leavers go with the blessing of Phoenix to serve elsewhere. The capacity of Phoenix Church to encourage people like this to follow the Spirit of Jesus is an important component of this kind of missional church ideology. It is most certainly required to really equip people to become missional disciple-makers in third places.

Yet others who have been interviewed, most of them indeed, have shared how they feel encouraged and empowered by the teaching to see themselves in a fresh way, as those called and sent. This theme of empowerment and encouragement is a very important qualitative measure to recognize in Phoenix Church. Leadership in Phoenix is not based on rigid hierarchical structures. They are structured to encourage every member to pursue what God is calling towards. I would suggest this is vital to any kind of leadership approach needed for effective missional transformation of an existing church. This most often requires a transition from an attractional maintenance-ministry mode of leadership, that is often hierarchical in nature, towards a missional-equipping community, which encourages and empowers people to participate. This seems to require a leadership structure that places leaders *alongside* rather than *above* members.

So Band-one people are those who feel encouraged and challenged to count the cost of engaging in the missio Dei. They may also feel challenged to count the cost of what this will mean in terms of their time commitments. It seems from an anecdotal point of view that they are attracted to the challenging and stirring atmosphere of Phoenix's Sunday services.

From a strategic point of view it seems important that missional churches offer a worship environment that is challenging people to go beyond their comfort zones, and to follow Christ at work ahead of them in their work places and neighborhoods. But also they need to offer effective pastoral support and care. This is another challenge Phoenix has faced. They have needed to keep on ensuring they are also properly caring for and supporting people. If the fivefold ministries are at work in Phoenix, then alongside the apostolic and prophetic call to follow the Christ of the gospel, there also needs to be good pastoral care. People need to be empowered and equipped with appropriate support, which is also at the center of the gospel of the grace and love of the Triune God. From this perspective missional churches also need to be healing therapeutic communities, where Christ can be encountered regularly. Research in Phoenix highlights the need for much more of this kind of pastoral support. It will surely strengthen what God is calling it to do. Counting the cost will also require good mentoring and counselling of an appropriate kind. Phoenix is becoming increasingly good at doing this among its members.

Band Two: Those Seeking to Be Equipped

Phoenix Church has changed in what Warner terms its axis from being a crucicentric/biblicist church, towards a conversionist/activist church.[9] Warner relates how evangelical churches that profile in terms of the first axis are normally more traditional and quite Calvinistic in their theological focus. They tend to be more inward-looking and not so readily outwardly focused in terms of their missional engagement with larger society. In terms of the latter profile, there is a tendency for churches like this to be much

---

9. Warner, *Reinventing English Evangelicalism* 1966–2001.

more open to an outward focus on mission, rather than on trying to keep the church safe from disruptive outside corrupting influences. Phoenix Church has most certainly moved from the former to the latter profile category. This has had an impact on the congregation.

It has led to the challenges mentioned under band one, related to a need to strengthen pastoral care as a much more costly missional gospel message is presented to people. The kinds of newer members who have joined the church since missional change began in Phoenix are those who are much more secure in their own faith identity. They seem to be much less fearful of losing their Christian identity when they seek to share their faith with others. They are also much more comfortable with new people joining the church. A cost for Phoenix is that it may mean that it will not be attractive for the traditional marginalized and vulnerable, who have largely been the traditional focus of evangelical social capital. We argue, however, that we also need to be relevant to the new marginalized. Both/and rather than either/or is the best kind of outcome Phoenix aims for. This has led to an exodus from Phoenix of those who come from what might be termed the more Reformed Calvinistic axis.

Some have bravely remained, and are actually embracing the change and are being transformed by it. Some remain and seek to tolerate the new way of life in Phoenix. This can be costly if it causes frustrations and tensions to exist between members who want different things. A cost of missional change has been revealed in my research by the change in axis in present-day Phoenix. The more recent missional-church focus is profiling for, and attracting, those who are comfortable with change. These profiled categories seem to count for the perceived cost of change. Hence, an ongoing theme of missional change at Phoenix is that people are encouraged to pursue training in the church's training school, as well as to become active local missionaries. Not all members from old Phoenix's way of life want this, some have left and others remain seeking to tolerate the new missional way of life and focus.

In interviews with members who fit this category, it was very clear that they were inspired and felt challenged to be equipped to serve Christ in this way. It was inspiring for me to hear also the brave accounts of how those who had been part of a much different church of the past were also seeking to be equipped for service. It had not been part of their original journey. They did not grow up in the church expecting these changes and neither did they join it with the expectation things would change as they now have. Indeed, some participants shared how in the years prior to the fire they had considered they had little to offer in terms of being able to lead others to Christ.

They had in those days sought to bring interested friends to visitor services at the church to hear the professional preacher share the gospel. Their accounts of personal transformation towards where they now see themselves, as needing to be equipped to participate in the missio Dei, are important testimony to the effectiveness of missional transformation that has been taking place in Phoenix. It has been a rather long journey. It will remain ongoing as mission never stops and neither does the equipping of the people of God to continue to be missionaries. Hence, this is a vital insight coming out of the research from which we can learn much.

Band Three: Those Being Equipped

Quite a number of the 70 percent in this church are seemingly being equipped for service in a variety of ways, including being mentored in on-the-job mission projects in the neighborhood. This does not imply all people in this category are doing the training courses. Etienne Wenger discusses the importance of "communities of practice."[10] By the participation of people in them they may take on the deeper values, beliefs, and convictions of those who form them. Wenger writes not as a practical theologian, but as a sociologist. His insights are important to any practical or empirical theological account, such as in this research account.

10. Wenger, *Communities of Practice*.

Meaning just lies beneath the surface of any intentional community of practice, including missional communities and their community-development projects in a neighborhood. People, by their very participation in the missional projects of Phoenix, may learn by association the deeper missional meanings that lie beneath the surface of these projects. Too little attention has been paid in the past to how *practices* transform and educate the people of God. Too much emphasis has been conversely placed on the preaching of the rational word, especially in evangelical churches, which impacts people little compared to participation in missional practices that are rich in theological meaning.

The missional café that Keith has discussed is passing on to its helpers the values and consciousness that God is at work in the world among them. This is a vital part of any missional transformation process for us to all learn from. This has also been an important finding in my research with Phoenix. The training school is not the only strategy being used to disciple God's people and other faith-seekers to become authentic followers of the missionary Spirit of Jesus. Any church does a disservice to people who have not come to faith by refusing to allow them to participate in projects it is engaged in, if they are not trained to do so. On-the-job training is very much part of what is encouraged at Phoenix. On-the-job training is too often underestimated and misunderstood. Arguably the Spirit of Christ is at work even in our practices to bring to consciousness the deeper hidden meaning of his Spirit's work within them.

Moving attention to the training school of Phoenix, a number of those engaged in it make up those who do not simply learn new ideas, but they too are placed in communities and projects of missional practice. I want to share an innovation that I have already brought to training for leaders in the programs I have innovated at ForMission College. They are based around five formation categories that make up reflexive-practice components of holistic formation on our BA and MA courses. These are also integrated into the Phoenix training school for ordinary church members to learn. They have proved effective to the missional leaders who work at

Phoenix. Some of those who were interviewed for my research clearly have learnt from these five formation categories.

Let's move on to the five formation outcomes that I think are vital for missional change to occur in any church undergoing missional transformation. They are:

Spiritual formation: to develop a listening posture and to learn how to better hear God's voice. To be enabled to discern what the missional Spirit of Jesus might be calling and sending each of us to do.

Missional formation: to develop well-informed missional practices that can be experimented with and reflected upon that actually enable people to become effective in participating in the ongoing mission of Jesus.

Ministry formation: part of God's call for all of God's people is participation in ministry and service (it is not a clerical function and it needs deconstructing from pertaining to clericalism).[11] It is part of the priesthood of all believers. Hence, every member in the body of Christ is called to serve God and others.

Personal formation: Christian characters need to be developed and transformed to become increasingly like that of Christ. We need to develop deep empathy with Christ and others. A goal needs to include ways and means that turn our attention to find out how our whole lives might be energized and infused with the person of Christ. In other words, we need to shape each other to have our own relationship with Christ, rather than making others dependent of another's faith to support them.

Intellectual formation: there is a proper place for head and heart to engage in dialogue, so that we might engage with

---

11. The so-called clerical paradigm used to train clergy has had the tendency to shape leaders best suited to serving ecclesiastical society rather than the real issues that everyday people face.

intellectual rigor in seeking to keep on exploring and understanding what God is revealing to us.

In research conducted at Phoenix there are those who have clearly been developing these important formation capacities to varying extents (in band three).

Band Four: Those Who Are Equipped

About 10 percent of the church have been equipped to serve and are now equipping others to do the same. Among those who have been equipped are leaders in the church who have completed ForMission College degree programs. They are passing on the DNA of the formation practices they have learnt. Importantly they are partnering with others who have been shaped and formed on the church's training courses. They are sharing leadership with these voluntary leaders. Phoenix has an eldership team who work with the pastor to help gauge the larger strategic issues they need to address as a missional community. The two leadership teams in the church are ten in number, made up of three elders, the pastor, and then the core leaders. They are male and female. They are all engaged in missional team ministry that intentionally seeks to shape the people of the congregation in their ongoing missional formation to differing extents.

It is important to recognize that the kind of gospel communicated by the leaders to Phoenix is the gospel of the kingdom. This is to be critically distinguished from the gospel of "my personal salvation," which has too often involved congregations consisting of members who claim to be "saved" but do not as such witness members making disciples of others. Our critique is that we believe that the early disciples were apprenticed in such a manner that they intentionally, and indeed quite naturally, sought to apprentice others to become allegiant followers of Christ. The gospel of the kingdom raises the stakes in terms of missio Dei theology.

Participation in the mission of the Triune God seems to call each of us to be more than simple consumers of personal salvation.

Perhaps the oft-repeated invitation for members to bring people to visitor services to hear the gospel has in fact fed a consumer gospel. This gospel product has seemingly often been neatly packaged by the trained experts and then sold to those who are ready to buy into it. However, we do not find the Christ of the Gospels peddling this kind of gospel. Rather, he seems to call for his followers to apprentice themselves to him in a developmental journey that takes several years. The so-called Great Commission of Matthew's Gospel[12] puts the imperative on making disciples who themselves become disciple-makers. The goal is not to bring people to church to hear the gospel, as such. It would seem to be much more about each believer apprenticing one or two to become authentic followers of Christ through life-on-life engagement with them in their everyday life contexts. The missional leadership team at Phoenix clearly appreciate how the gospel of the kingdom makes every believer a "sent-one" to make disciples of others.

There are other gospel versions being communicated in evangelical-Pentecostal-charismatic kinds of churches (EPCs). Bill Hull has done much to highlight them in his own work.[13] To name a couple of these other gospels, we might include, the prosperity gospel, the consumer gospel, the gospel of the left and right, and the gospel of the saved, or a kingdom-of-God gospel. For more discussion of these kinds of gospel typologies consider Hull's helpful contributions.

Becoming a Mission-Equipping Community

It must be recognized that all of what has been discussed in this chapter is part of an answer to the question of how to equip a faith-community to become something of a mission-equipping agent. What I have written is far from a comprehensive answer (if anyone could ever offer such).

---

12. Matt 28:16–20.
13. Hull, *Conversion and Discipleship*.

What I pick up next thematically are some suggestive matters of importance.[14] The four typologies/categories of members, suggested for Phoenix, actually seem to reveal some dynamics that might help to transform a congregation to become more incarnational. So let's trace these processes a bit more with reference to the typologies, as a means to reveal some potential dynamics required for missional-change management to occur similar to those emerging in Phoenix.

Obviously both writers express their core values by suggesting that they are convinced that what has been occurring in Phoenix is part of a work of the Spirit of God. Church members have been responding to the missional changes occurring in their congregation. Of course, no change process will take everyone with it. The missional process has been something that the congregation has continued to employ its leaders to help them to continue on this missional journey. This is important to any change process in terms of congregational structures of governance. A majority of congregational members need to be participants in any missional-change process. Change must be meaningfully perceived to be what God wants and thus what they as a community also want. It is well known that leaders soon lose their jobs if they evade the support of their congregations. Of course, at times it may be that a leader's vision for change outgrows the congregation that employ her or him. This requires a leader to discern this as part of what God might be calling her or him to move on to next.

The present senior leader at Phoenix is moving into his tenth year there. Hence, this speaks to the quality of his brand of leadership. In interviews with the leader and his team, it is evident that the whole missional change process has been a costly one of transformation for the church and its leaders. The church has chosen to keep going on with this process. I would fully agree that this costly journey comes across strongly in all my meetings with leaders and

14. For a much fuller articulation of how to form transformative communities that shape believers for participation in the missio Dei in third places Keith and my own doctoral research accounts will need to be consulted when they are finally published. This work is essentially an early view of a more popular kind prepared in advance of our later research theses.

in the accounts of those I have interviewed among members. This is a vital component of missional change, that the leaders must be authentic disciples of Christ themselves before they can disciple others. People soon sniff out a rat.

Also it is vital to hear the prophetic voice, and to be guided by it as part of any fivefold-ministries-shaped missional change process. If Christ is not leading ahead of the people of God, calling them to transcend their own human strategies and limiting horizons, then the church may soon become a club or a place where power games are played. In other words, abusive leadership structures where change is forced on congregations have at times been part of the tapestry of what some call missional church. We need to follow the real presence of Christ as his Spirit calls us to continue to participate in what he is calling us to do. This is dialectical missional theology. It is not simply based on a static deposit of received truth that needs to shape and inform a congregation's horizons for now and forevermore. It also needs to include a prophetic deposit receiving continuing revelations of what God is still calling his people to do in participation with the Spirit of Jesus. This means missional churches need to be based on a working operant spiritual theology, if they are to be enabled to continue to shape and form every member to become missionaries. Healthy missional communities seem to require the kind of leadership that actively listens out for the Spirit of Christ's voice among the people of these kinds of congregations.

My research with Phoenix Church has revealed some matters of importance regarding what is seemingly of relevance to shape and form missional congregations. Differing congregational contexts will require fresh innovative missional strategies in order for them to be effective. There is no one-size-fits-all typology. But hopefully we might sense something of the themes that may be of more universal importance from this short narrative. It is a humble suggestive contribution to the so-called missional conversation. In order for missional churches to really empower God's people for mission, they may need to discard old Christendom habits of a clericalism that seeks to exercise hierarchical authority over people. Perhaps we need to transition the sub-culture of our churches to move towards walking alongside people as Christ does and did.

This will not be the kind of leadership that some churches desire. Neither will it be the kind that denominations will necessarily want their ordained clergy to aver. It is costly and risky to have a more flexible openness to what the Spirit of Christ might be calling his people to participate in doing. If leaders cultivate the wrong kind of environment for these more flexible forms of missional openness to the Spirit, then it may have the effect of causing schisms and power struggles that are unhealthy within their congregations. However, we may need to seriously reflect on how we might address challenges that occur in dynastically structured churches. The problem here would likely be that ruling dynasties will limit and inhibit a more open and flexible kind of listening posture in a congregation. This kind of posture seems to be fundamental to any discernment to begin meaningful participation in the ongoing mission of the Spirit of Jesus. Are our congregations forming God's people to participate in God's mission in the Spirit's power with the message of his Son?[15] There are signs of a hopeful future. We need to make sure that we take the ordinary members of our churches on a journey to discern what God wants them to do alongside Christ.

---

15. This is claimed by Phoenix Church members interviewed to be the motto that has stuck and best describes what is occurring at Phoenix.

Conclusion

So What Now? A Hopeful Future

Keith Foster

Theological Reflection—God and the City

Creating places for the good and prosperity of the broader community and city, engaging the wider community (not just the measured marginalized), seeking to enhance the overall sense of community belonging and well-being, all within an intentional gospel framework, have been the challenge and focus of this book. As we conclude our considerations, what might theological reflection reveal in such areas? One of the four key tenets of evangelicalism is *biblicism*, a high regard for the authority of the Bible to inform all of life and praxis. Out of such a tradition, it will be important to underpin any theories and projects with solid biblical and theological reflection that informs any subsequent response of the evangelical, urban, community-facing church.

Isaiah and Jeremiah are good places to start with regards reflections around attitudes and approaches to the city. Jeremiah 29:7 exhorts the exiles to "Seek the welfare of the city into which you have been called, for in its welfare you will find your welfare."

Hjalmarson considers this whole aspect of seeking the welfare or "shalom" of the city, seeing it much more than simply the absence of conflict, but rather the "wholeness and prosperity, peace and justice—a community that is thriving in relationship to the Creator and to the land."[1] Jeremiah in the preceding verses gives practical examples of what that might look like for God's people, "Build houses . . . plant gardens . . . eat their produce."[2] In effect, create places where God's kingdom can flourish and be visible. All of this "activity" is to be underpinned with prayer on behalf of the whole city.[3]

Isaiah 65:17–25 gives a picture of the sort of city (according to Hjalmarson) that God himself promises to build. The Lord's New Jerusalem will be a place of joy, house building, sowing, and reaping. As the urban-facing church seeks to create such places within the city, the sowing, reaping, and building may be more metaphorical in the sense of sowing seeds of faith, reaping friendships and lives that are transformed, building communities of hope and flourishing.

Many churches may indeed seek to create such places within their own buildings and church programs. However, John 1:14 reminds us that God's primary strategy was one of incarnation as, "the Word became flesh and dwelt amongst us." Rumsey points here to the Trinitarian nature of God, as God moves "toward humanity," all of this taking place "where we really are."[4] God reveals himself in real places to real people. John's Gospel commences with this remarkable claim of the knowable Logos coming, being, and dwelling amongst us. While John reflects upon the reality of rejection, there are, and will be, those that recognize and respond.[5] Contrary to our natural and understandable desire as God's people to remain within our tribes and comfortable places, the Gospels and Acts reveal God's people as those who are subject to tensions

1. Hjalmarson, *No Home Like Place*, 159.
2. Jer 29:5.
3. Jer 29:7.
4. Rumsey, *Parish*, 19–20.
5. John 1:11–12.

caused by the divine-human interactions. Tension created as they are challenged to see beyond their informed text (Peter in Acts 10). Tension as they are encouraged to emulate their master and incarnate into the messy places (Jesus sending out the seventy-two in Luke 10). Tension as they are instructed to declare the kingdom of God.[6] Someone has said that "Jesus preached the kingdom and got the church." While this might be an understandable and memorable saying, borne out of the many frustrations one can experience in mobilizing the church to fulfill its kingdom mandate, I believe in the church. Paul tells us that it is "through the church that the glorious mystery of the gospel is announced and made known."[7] The church as the bride of Christ is in preparation, in what Newbigin so beautifully described as the hermeneutic of the gospel. When the church works and is empowered and in tune with the Spirit to fulfill its mission and purpose, even the "rulers and authorities in the heavenly realms" are enlightened and amazed. What a glorious gospel we have!

So, who might this glorious gospel be for? Considering the default approach of many churches, perhaps just the poor and needy might be the focus. The Bible certainly gives plenty of examples of the inclusion and importance of the marginalized of society. Yet John 1:12 tells us that, "to all who did receive him . . . he gave the right to be called children of God." While Jesus highlighted the hardness of the rich with regards to openness to the kingdom,[8] Luke goes on to carefully position the account of the salvation of Zacchaeus in the next section of his Gospel.[9] Jesus does not express his kingdom mandate to be aimed at the rich or poor but rather "the lost."[10]

An all-inclusive mandate for the urban-facing church to create gospel-places for the whole community outside of welfare provision would guard against a narrowing of Jesus' kingdom

6. Luke 10:9.
7. Eph 3:10.
8. Luke 18:18–25.
9. Luke 19:1–10.
10. Luke 19:10.

manifesto. John Inge relates place to that of "ultimate hope." According to Inge, places where God is talked about and faith is lived out are a reflection of our ultimate eschatological hope.[11] Jesus goes to "prepare a place for [us]."[12] God's people look forward to the new place, the "new city" where "there will be no more death, mourning, crying or pain."[13] The church in the city can provide a foretaste of a gospel and kingdom hermeneutic; their lived lives on display as an example of what it means to serve King Jesus within incarnational ways might include eschatological expressions of hope and kingdom come.

As the church continues to face the challenges of relevance and inclusion in what some have termed the post-secular city, my hope is that this book has highlighted, in some way, the huge opportunity for the church to do more than simply "contribute." The church has much more to offer than simply to fill the welfare gap of local governments and welfare providers. I would argue that the church is the "hope of the world." With millions of volunteers motivated by a spiritual capitalist desire to seek the "prosperity of the city," including above all its spiritual prosperity, the church is well placed to position itself within the urban landscape as a voice of hope and reason.

Just as one small café in the West Midlands is starting to create a place of enhanced community and faith exploration for the local people, each church (at least within the evangelical tradition) that desires the good of its city should seek to provide an "oasis" of hope. Such an oasis needs to model the kind of community that welcomes faith-seekers with an unashamed gospel intentionality. They will need to work with people without prejudice among both the marginalized and the "perceived" unmarginalized.

---

11. Inge, *A Christian Theology of Place*, 139.
12. John 14:4.
13. Rev 21:4.

Appendix

Does the New Testament Expect All Believers to Engage in Mission?

A good critique of a major assumption we make in this book is that it is not obvious from reading the Gospels, Acts, or Paul's writings that all believers are expected to become disciple-makers. We acknowledge this critique, with some observations that need to be taken into account. Firstly, biblical evidence that provides at least some indication that all believers are called to become disciple-makers will be discussed. Secondly, we want to make some qualifications of how this claim that every believer is called to missionary discipleship might be understood to work in practice.

Longenecker's et al. scholarly contributions on the topic of discipleship in the New Testament is recommended to help provide a more in-depth consideration of the importance and role of discipleship in the New Testament documents.[14] Two fundamental matters are worth noting from this work. Firstly, the authors of the volume argue that discipleship is assumed by the New Testament writers to be normative for *every* Christian. Longenecker comments: "Outside the four Gospels, the Acts, and the one or two instances in the Apocalypse, . . . 'disciple' and 'follower' are conspicuously absent in the rest of the New Testament." However, he argues, that the language of "disciple," "follower," or "to be, or become a disciple" is implied in the rhetoric of the letters

14. Longenecker, ed. *Patterns of Discipleship in the New Testament.*

Appendix

and occasional writings beyond the Gospels and Acts. He suggests that "concepts of imitation, example, or patterning, or statements and exhortations regarding authentic Christian existence" are the language used to shape and form those assumed to be disciples in the churches that writers like Paul address.[15]

Hence, Longenecker et al. argue that the occasional letters of Paul assume that believers are being shaped as followers of Christ in their churches.[16] However, differing kinds of rhetoric are used in each letter to articulate what this shaping and forming process needs to look like, suited to the context of the churches to which the letters were written.

However, can it be claimed that every believer is positioned in the accounts of the Gospels, or the book of Acts, to become disciples *who then should seek to make disciples of others*? Surely, to use this language, "to make disciples," arises from Matthew 28:16–20. And is that command not directed to the apostles of Christ? First of all, a careful reading of Matthew 28:16–20 indicates that only the eleven remaining "disciples" met with Christ in Galilee on the occasion of the giving of the so called "Great Commission." It is interesting that Matthew does not use the word "apostles," but rather "disciples" in this passage. I would suggest that a reason for this is because he did not want to give the impression that only the apostles were sent to make disciples of the nations. It was his intention to position every believer in Christ to become a disciple-maker. Given that in Matthew 10, Matthew used the word "apostles" for the twelve, it must be significant that he does *not* use it in Matthew 28. If he had only wanted the apostles to be the ones sent to make disciples then surely he would have used the already-accepted category descriptor "apostles" to emphasize their special role as disciple-makers.

Matthew's account must not be taken in isolation in the Synoptic tradition. Luke 10 suggests seventy others were sent to make disciples, although the language to "make" is not used there, it is implied. Moreover, Acts one suggests there were 120 followers of

---

15. Longenecker, ed., *Patterns of Discipleship in the New Testament*, 5.
16. Longenecker, ed., *Patterns of Discipleship in the New Testament*, 5.

Christ prior to the outpouring of the Spirit, who prayerfully awaited for power from on high to engage in mission. Given the early nature of the Christian mission, that framed the context of these documents, it is natural to assume that a core group of apostles and disciples were prepared by Christ to shape yet other disciples to do the same in what followed in the ongoing mission of Jesus, after his ascension. Hence, at least by way of implication, it might be argued that in order for the church to continue to participate in the ongoing mission of the Spirit of Jesus, new believers were positioned to become disciples *and disciple-makers* themselves, when they were ready to do it. However, in the early context of the Christian mission, it was vital to place the apostles and existing disciples (the 120) as the examples of authentic discipleship on which to model later discipleship formation. I would suggest every believer is to become a disciple like those early apostles and disciples.

Nevertheless, it is fair for readers to raise the critique that the language of "making disciples" is Matthean language. I would suggest that, given that this language concludes the Gospel of Matthew, as part of a climactic command, it would not make for a common-sense interpretation of this language to suggest that "to make disciples" would only be the work of eleven men.

We should note carefully that the disciples are to "make disciples of all nations, baptizing them in the name of the Father and of the Son and of the Holy Spirit, and *teaching them to obey everything I have commanded you.*" Now one of the things Jesus commanded the eleven, which they are to pass on to the disciples they make, is *this very command here,* to make disciples of all nations! Thus, this great commission includes a command to make disciples *who themselves make disciples.*

In the later church, it must surely have required more than the apostles to make disciples, or the Christian mission would have failed. Indeed, one might argue that the genius of Jesus' discipleship-making strategy is that every believer can readily relate to the ordinary men and women (in Luke's account) who became followers of Jesus. Hence, all the ordinary women and men might come to think of themselves as disciples and disciple-makers like the first followers. It is my view, that later believers who read the account of Matthew 28 should position themselves, as social actors, in the place of the eleven disciples of Matthew 28:16. Readers and listeners would naturally position themselves to become disciple-makers like the eleven. Hence, the rest of the Matthean account, with its teaching sections focused on discipleship and apostleship, is meant to apply to every believer, as they are shaped as followers of Christ similar to the first followers. I would also argue that this is true for the other Gospels too, generally speaking.

For example, how do we make sense of the Gospels as documents themselves? What is their purpose? As a missiologist, I would suggest they make best sense as missionary documents. In other words, these written accounts of the words and works of Jesus, and the life of his disciples and apostles, make best sense as sources designed to continue to inform the missionary Christian movement of what missionary disciples-who-make-disciples need to become. Future disciples are to be shaped by the Gospel tradition of Jesus to follow the Spirit of Jesus,[17] participating in his ongoing mission. They are called to continue to follow the real presence of their Master still at work in the world, whom they are being shaped to follow. All four Gospels would seem to make best sense in this way. But particularly in the case of Matthew's Gospel, every disciple is in principle, at least, placed as a social actor as a follower and disciple-maker.

If you agree with this broad assumption, that I feel makes best sense of the Gospels as missionary documents, then every believer is called to share their faith with others and to make disciples.

We need to make some qualifying statements to nuance this line of thought, to put some cautions in place. Firstly, the Gospels have remained normative sources of theological authority for the church throughout the centuries. However, they have been interpreted in different ways. So in the first three centuries, they make best sense as missionary-guiding documents (indeed the same applies in subsequent centuries). The church was engaged in missionary expansion from the edges of society to the center.

17. Acts 16:6–10.

Moreover, the way in which discipleship was understood in the first-century context changed in the second century (and onwards) as the church began to seek to consolidate its communities. The authority of bishops and authorized leaders became paramount to save the church from corruption, due to heresies like Gnosticism. Hence, leaders increasingly became the primary disciple-makers. However, this does not challenge my earlier argument, that the Gospels particularly position each person, who reads or listens to the Gospel stories, as followers to be shaped by the teaching of Lord Jesus.

Secondly, the Gospels themselves make a distinction between the crowds who followed Jesus, but were not as yet his disciples, and a broader group of disciples sent out on mission, such as the seventy disciples of Luke 10, and the apostles (Matthew 10). The example from Luke 10 presents disciples other than the apostles as what might be termed disciple-makers. The point I really want to focus on here, is that groups like the "crowds" were not yet allegiant followers of Christ. In order for them to give their allegiance to Jesus, they would need to first of all be shaped to become effective faithful followers of Christ. This is true in the contemporary situation of the church. Not everyone who comes to church is ready to become a disciple-maker. They will first of all need to be discipled themselves to become a true follower who can remain faithful to Christ. However, if they do become a faithful follower of Christ, then I would suggest they would naturally fit with my earlier suggestion, that the Gospel's as missionary documents assume they will become disciple-makers themselves.

Thirdly, it is important to qualify this language, that suggests that everyone who is a disciple of Christ needs to be a disciple-maker. It is not possible for all believers to always act as disciple-makers. For example, if they face serious illness, then this may change their priorities. Moreover, not everyone is called to leadership. Leadership in the way we understand it here is that leaders themselves need to develop structures in missional churches to equip every believer to be a disciple-maker. Each of us have a calling on our lives, which I believe includes what we do for a

Appendix

career. Having said this, it does seem evident that each believer is to seek to discern how to share their faith with others and then to make disciples of them. I believe it is important to make this qualification.

Fourthly, it is not straightforward to argue that Paul has nothing to say about discipleship. This is why it is important to read something like Longenecker's edited work, to give a much more nuanced and detailed account of the Pauline corpus on this subject. Having said this, Paul's occasional letters do not, for the most part, make the case for believers to act as disciple-makers. It is important to recognize that letters like that to the Romans, or that addressed to the Galatians, are more concerned with an apologetic for Paul's gospel theology. 1 and 2 Thessalonians are focused on matters to do with cultural challenges, to do with the resurrection of the dead and the second coming of Christ, rather than missionary activities of the churches. 1 Corinthians seeks to deal with the disunity and factions within the church of Corinth. It is seeking to address the way of life in this young church community. It does not as such seek to focus on mission in broader terms. However, it is true that Paul positions himself as their apostle, sent to guide them to properly address the challenges of being a community, that might then become mature enough to represent Christ and to became an agency of discipleship. I think that the letters of Paul, are first of all, seeking to develop the believing communities to which he writes, rather than positioning members within them as disciple-makers. They need to be shaped and formed for faithful service before they can properly serve and make disciples of others.

Fifthly, Carsten Peter Thiede has made an excellent point about the lack of Paul's use of stories like those found in the Gospels in his letters to these young churches.[18] He argued that Paul assumed that the churches he wrote to had accounts of the life and ministry of Jesus recounted to them regularly, often at first, as oral testimony delivered to them by eyewitnesses. The suggestion here is that Paul did not consider it necessary to give accounts of the Gospel stories, because they were regularly being communicated

---

18. Thiede, *Jesus Life or Legend?*

to these congregations. And it follows, that one of the central motifs of the four Gospels was Jesus' instruction on discipleship. Hence, I would suggest that Paul expected these kinds of Gospel accounts to shape disciples in each of the new churches that had been planted. It was not required for him to retell these stories in his occasional letters to these churches. For these reasons, I believe that discipleship and the making of disciples is implied in the New Testament documents beyond the Gospels and Acts. But it is not expressed in disciple-making language for the reasons I highlight.

We suggest then that all believers should come to see themselves as disciple-making disciples of Christ.

Bibliography

Amess, Robert. *Healing the Body of Christ: Restoring Hope and Calm to a Fragmented Church.* Milton Keynes, UK: Authentic, 2007.
Astin, Howard. *Body and Cell: Making the Transition to Cell Church a First-Hand Account.* Grand Rapids: Monarch, 2002.
Astley, Jeff, and Leslie J. Francis, eds. *Exploring Ordinary Theology: Everyday Christian Believing and the Church.* Farnham, UK: Ashgate, 2013.
Astley, Jeff. *Ordinary Theology: Looking, Listening and Learning in Theology.* Farnham, UK: Ashgate, 2002.
Baker, Chris. "Spiritual Capital and Progressive Localism." Public Spirit Blog, 2014. Online: https://www.academia.edu/7462548/Spiritual_Capital_and_Progressive_Localism.
Baker, Chris, and Jonathan Miles-Watson. "Exploring Secular Spiritual Capital: An Engagement in Religious and Secular Dialogue for a Common Future?" *International Journal of Public Theology* 2 (2008) 442–64.
Baker, C., and H. Skinner. *Faith in Action, The Dynamic Connection between Spiritual and Religious Capital.* Manchester: William Temple Foundation, 2005.
Beasley-Murray, G. R. *Jesus and the Kingdom of God.* Carlisle, UK: Paternoster, 1986.
Beaumont, Justin, and Chris Baker, eds. *Postsecular Cities, Space, Theory and Practice.* London: Continuum, 2011.
Bebbington, D. W. *Evangelicalism in Modern Britain: A History from the 1730s to the 1980s.* London: Routledge, 2005.
Bennett, Z., and A. Rogers. *Report on Bible and Practical Theology Symposium.* Birmingham, UK: BIAPT, 2012.
Bockmuehl, Klaus. *Listening to the God Who Speaks.* Colorado Springs: Helmers and Howard, 1990.
Bonhoeffer, D. *The Cost of Discipleship.* New York: Touchstone, 1995.
Bosch, David. J. *Transforming Mission: Paradigm Shifts in Theology of Mission.* Maryknoll, NY: Orbis, 2000.
Bourdieu, Pierre. "The Forms of Capital." In *Handbook of Theory and Research for the Sociology of Education*, edited by John G. Richardson, 241–58. New York: Greenwood, 1986.

Brown, David. "A Sacramental World: Why it Matters." In *The Oxford Handbook of Sacramental Theology*, edited by Hans Boersma and Matthew Levering, 603–15. Oxford: Oxford University, 2015.

Byrne, Brendon. *The Hospitality of God: A Reading of Luke's Gospel*. Collegeville, MN: Liturgical, 2015.

Cartledge, Mark. "The Use of Scripture in Practical Theology: A Study of Academic Practice." *Practical Theology* 6 (2013) 271–83.

Castells, Manuel. *The Power of Identity: The Information Age—Society, and Culture*. Vol. 2. Chichester, UK: Wiley-Blackwell, 2004.

Chester, Tim. *Good News to the Poor*. Nottingham, UK: IVP, 2004.

Cloke, Paul, Justin Beaumont, and A. Williams. *Working Faith: Faith-Based Organisations and Urban Social Justice*. Milton Keynes, UK: Paternoster, 2013.

Cloke, Paul, and Mike Pears, eds. *Mission in Marginal Places: The Theory*. Milton Keynes, UK: Paternoster, 2016.

Coleman, John. "Social Capital in the Creation of Human Capital." *American Journal of Sociology* 94 (1988) 95–120.

Croft, Steven. *Transforming Communities: Re-imagining the Church for the 21st Century*. London: Darton Longman and Todd, 2002.

Deere, Jack. *Surprised by the Voice of God: How God Speaks to Us Today*. Eastbourne, UK: Kingsway, 1997.

Drane, John. *Do Christians Know How to be Spiritual? The Rise of New Spirituality and the Mission of the Church*. London: Darton Longman and Todd, 2005.

Egan, G. *The Skilled Helper*. 10th ed. Belmont, CA: Brooks/Cole, 2010.

Fee, Gordon. *Paul, the Spirit and the People of God*. London: Hodder and Stoughton, 1997.

Fiddes, Paul. *Participating in God: A Pastoral Doctrine of the Trinity*. Louisville, KY: Westminster, John Knox, 2000.

Flett, John. *The Witness of God: The Trinity, Missio Dei, Karl Barth, and the Nature of Christian Community*. Grand Rapids: Eerdmans, 2010.

Foster, C. *Wired for God? The Biology of Spiritual Experience*. London: Hodder and Stoughton, 2010.

Frost, Michael, and Alan Hirsch. *The Shaping of Things to Come: Innovation and Mission for the 21st Century Church*. Rev. ed. Grand Rapids: Baker, 2013.

George, Timothy. *Theology of the Reformers*. Nashville: Broadman, 1988.

Graham, Elaine, and Stephen Lowe. *What Makes a Good City? Public Theology and the Urban Church*. London: Darton, Longman and Todd, 2009.

Groothuis, Douglas. *Christian Apologetics: A Comprehensive Case for Biblical Faith*. Downers Grove, IL: IVP Academic, 2011.

Habermas, Jürgen. "Secularism's Crisis of Faith: Notes on Post-Secular Society." *New Perspectives Quarterly* 25 (2008) 16–29.

Hardy, Alister. *The Spiritual Nature of Man*. Oxford: Clarendon, 1979.

Hardy, Andrew. "How a Ministerial Education Programme with a Very Distinctive Ethos Has Helped Leaders to Begin to Develop a New Living

Bibliography

Tradition in a Church." Unpublished paper, Roehampton University, 2016.

———. *Pictures of God: Shaping Missional Church Life*. Watford, UK: Instant Apostle, 2016.

Hardy, Andrew, and Dan Yarnell. *Forming Multicultural Partnerships: Church Planting in a Divided Society*. Watford, UK: Instant Apostle, 2015.

———. *Missional Discipleship After Christendom*. Eugene, OR: Cascade, 2018.

Hardy, Andrew, Richard Whitehouse, and Dan Yarnell. *Power and the Powers: The Use and Abuse of Power in the Missional Context*. Eugene, OR: Cascade, 2015.

Hicks, John Mark. *Come to the Table: Revisioning the Lord's Supper*. Fairmont, VA: Leafwood, 2002.

Hill, Graham, ed. *Signs of Hope in the City: Renewing Urban Mission, Embracing Radical Hope*. Australia: ISUM and Micah, 2015.

Hjalmarson, Leonard. *No Home Like Place: A Christian Theology of Place*. Portland, OR: Urban Loft, 2015.

Holliday, Adrian, Martin Hyde, and John Kullman. *Intercultural Communication: An Advanced Resource Book for Students*. 2nd ed. London: Routledge, 2010.

Holmes, Peter. R. *Trinity in Human Community: Exploring Congregational Life in the Image of the Social Trinity*. Milton Keynes, UK: Paternoster, 2006.

Holmes, Peter. R., and Susan B. Williams. *Becoming More Like Christ: A Contemporary Biblical Journey*. Milton Keynes, UK: Paternoster, 2007.

Hull, Bill. *Conversion and Discipleship: You Can't Have One without the Other*. Grand Rapids: Zondervan, 2016.

Inge, John. *A Christian Theology of Place*. Farnham, UK: Ashgate, 2003.

Karkkainen, Veli-Matti. *One with God: Salvation as Deification and Justification*. Collegeville, MN: Liturgical, 2004.

———. *Pneumatology: The Holy Spirit in Ecumenical, International, and Contextual Perspective*. Grand Rapids: Baker Academic, 2002.

Longenecker, R. N., ed. *Patterns of Discipleship in the New Testament*. Grand Rapids: Eerdmans, 1996.

Manzo, John. *Machines, People and Social Interaction in Third Wave Coffeehouses, Calgary*. Calgary, AB: University of Calgary, 2014.

Moltmann, Jürgen. *The Crucified God*. London: SCM, 2001.

———. *God in Creation: An Ecological Doctrine of Creation*. London: SCM, 1985.

———. *Theology of Hope*. London: SCM, 2002.

———. *The Trinity and the Kingdom of God*. London: SCM, 1981.

Moynagh, Michael, and Philip Harrold. *Church for Every Context: An Introduction to Theology and Practice*. London: SCM, 2012.

Newberg, Andrew, and Mark Waldam. *How God Changes Your Brain: Breakthrough Findings from a Leading Neuroscientist*. New York: Ballatine, 2009.

Bibliography

Newbigin, Lesslie. *The Gospel in a Pluralist Society*. Grand Rapids: Eerdmans, 1989.

———. *Lesslie Newbigin Missionary Theologian: A Reader*. Edited by Paul Weston. Grand Rapids: Eerdmans, 2006.

———. *The Open Secret: An Introduction to the Theology of Mission*. London: SPC, 1995.

Neyrey, Jerome H., ed. *The Social World of Luke-Acts: Models for Interpretation*. Peabody, MA: Hendrickson, 2005.

Oldenburg, Ray. *The Great Good Place, Cafes, Coffee Shops, Bookstores, Bars, Hair Salons and Other Hangouts at the Heart of a Community*. Cambridge: MA: Da Capo, 1999.

Office of National Statistics. Online: https://www.ons.gov.uk/.

Ott, Craig, Stephen J. Strauss, and Timothy C. Tennent. *Encountering Theology of Mission: Biblical Foundations, Historical Developments, and Contemporary Issues*. Grand Rapids: Baker Academic, 2010.

Pattison, Stephen. *The Challenge of Practical Theology*. London: Kingsley, 2007.

Pickle, Bob. "The Word Church in the Old Testament." Online: http://www.pickle-publishing.com/papers/church-in-old-testament.htm. Accessed, 12 December 2018.

Pitman, Elizabeth. *Transactional Analysis for Social Workers and Counsellors: An Introduction*. London: Tavistock/Routledge, 1990.

Power, Anne, and Helen Willmot. *Social Capital within the Neighbourhood*. Case report 38. London: Centre for Analysis of Social Exclusion, 2007.

Putnam, Robert. *Bowling Alone: The Collapse and Revival of American Community*. New York: Simon and Schuster, 2001.

Robinson, William. *The Biblical Doctrine of the Church*. 1948. Reprint, Eugene, OR: Wipf and Stock, 1997.

Ross, Kathy, and Steven B. Bevans, eds. *Mission on the Road to Emmaus: Constants, Context, and Prophetic Dialogue*. Maryknoll, NY: Orbis, 2015.

Roxburgh, Alan J., and Fred Romanuk. *The Missional Leader: Equipping Your Church to Reach a Changing World*. San Francisco: Jossey-Bass, 2006.

Rumsey, Andrew. *Parish: An Anglican Theology of Place*. London: SCM, 2017.

Sedgwick, Peter, ed. *God in the City: Essays and Reflections from the Archbishop of Canterbury's Urban Theology Group*. London: Mowbray, 1995.

Sheldrake, Philip. *Spaces for the Sacred*. London: SCM, 2001.

Smith, James. K. A. *Desiring the Kingdom: Worship, Worldview, and Cultural Formation*. Vol. 1. Grand Rapids: Baker Academic, 2009.

———. *Imagining the Kingdom: How Worship Works*. Vol 2. Grand Rapids: Baker Academic, 2013.

Stackhouse, Max. L. "Ethics and Eschatology." In *The Oxford Handbook of Eschatology*, edited by Jerry L. Walls, 548–62. Oxford: Oxford University, 2008.

Stevens, Paul. R. *The Abolition of the Laity: Vocation, Work and Ministry in a Biblical Perspective*. Milton Keynes, UK: Paternoster, 2006.

Bibliography

Stoddard, Chris, and Nick Cuthbert. *Church on the Edge: Principles and Real Life Stories*. Milton Keynes, UK: Authentic, 2006.

Tennent, Timothy. C. *Invitation to World Missions: A Trinitarian Missiology for the Twenty-first Century*. Grand Rapids: Kregel, 2010.

Thiede, C. P. *Jesus Life or Legend?* Oxford: Lion, 1997.

Thwaites, James. *The Church beyond the Congregation*. Milton Keynes, UK: Paternoster, 1999.

Van Gelder, Craig. *The Missional Church in Context: Helping Congregations Develop Contextual Ministry*. Grand Rapids: Baker Academic, 2007.

Ward, Pete. *Introducing Practical Theology: Mission, Ministry, and the Life of the Church*. Grand Rapids: Baker Academic, 2017.

———. *Liquid Ecclesiology: The Gospel and the Church*. Leiden: Brill, 2017.

———. *Participation and Mediation: A Practical Theology for the Liquid Church*. London: SCM, 2008.

Warner, Rob. *Reinventing English Evangelicalism, 1966–2001: A Theological and Sociological Study*. Studies in Evangelical History and Thought. Milton Keynes, UK: Paternoster, 2007.

Wenger, Etienne. *Communities of Practice: Learning, Meaning, and Identity*. Cambridge: Cambridge University Press, 2016.

Wright, Christopher. J. H. *The Mission of God's People: A Biblical Theology of the Church's Mission*. Grand Rapids: Zondervan, 2010.

Wright, N. T. *Paul: Fresh Perspectives*. London: SPCK, 2005.

Zizioulas, John. D. *Being as Communion*. London: Darton Longman and Todd, 2013.

———. *The Eucharistic Communion and the World*. London: T. & T. Clark, 2011.

Printed in Great
Britain
by Amazon